☐☐☐☐☐☐☐☐

TEACHING AND LEARNING
EARLY NUMBER

D0089101

TEACHING AND LEARNING
EARLY NUMBER

Edited by
Ian Thompson

Open University Press
Buckingham · Philadelphia

Open University Press
Celtic Court
22 Ballmoor
Buckingham
MK18 1XW

and
1900 Frost Road, Suite 101
Bristol, PA 19007, USA

First Published 1997

A catalogue record of this book is available from the British Library

ISBN   0 335 19851 1 (pb)   0 335 19852 X (hb)

Library of Congress Cataloging-in-Publication Data
Teaching and learning early number / Ian Thompson (ed.).
      p. cm.
   Includes bibliographical references (p. –) and indexes.
   ISBN 0–335–19852–X (hb). — ISBN 0–335–19851–1 (pb)
      1. Mathematics—Study and teaching (Primary)—Great Britain.
   I. Thompson. Ian (Frederick Ian)
   QA135.5.T398   1997
   372.7'2—dc21
                                                        96–49718
                                                          CIP

Typeset by Graphicraft Typesetters Ltd., Hong Kong
Printed in Great Britain by St Edmundsbury Press Ltd.,
Bury St Edmunds, Suffolk

Contents

Notes on contributors

Carol Aubrey is a senior lecturer in the School of Education at the University of Durham. A major research interest has been the investigation of the informal mathematical knowledge that young children bring into school and teachers' pedagogical subject knowledge. This has led to the award of an ESRC grant which is soon to be reported in *The Processes of Mathematical Instruction in Children's First Year at School*. Sponsored by The British Council, she is currently investigating children's mental methods of calculation for ages 6–12 years, in collaboration with the University of Ljubljana, Slovenia.

Julia Anghileri is head of mathematics at Homerton College, Cambridge and has published a number of articles in professional and research journals relating to children learning arithmetic. She has extensive experience with both pre-service and in-service teachers through undergraduate and post-graduate courses as well as in-service courses. She is actively involved in research into children's learning of arithmetic. Her PhD dissertation was entitled 'Young children's understanding of multiplication' (1988).

Janet Duffin was a secondary teacher of mathematics before moving into teacher education, where she became involved with both initial and in-service training. She took a particular interest in mathematics at the primary level because of its importance as a foundation for future learning. She was Evaluator to the CAN (Calculator Aware Number) component of the PrIME (Primary Initiatives in Mathematics Education) Project while also working with non-mathematics undergraduates who needed to become more numerate in preparation for employment. Her research interests are in the development of a theory of learning aimed at supporting the teaching of mathematics at every level. She is a member of the Advisory Group for the National Numeracy Project.

Sue Gifford is senior lecturer in mathematics education at the Roehampton Institute, London. She has worked in a variety of inner-London schools as a teacher and mathematics consultant. Her current interests include the mathematical education of nursery children.

Eddie Gray is a senior lecturer in mathematical education in the Institute of Education at the University of Warwick. He is Director of the Mathematics Education Research Centre. His 20 years' teaching experience within schools, of which 5 years were as a headteacher in Bournemouth, covers both primary and secondary phases. His current research interests continue to focus on success and failure in mathematics and recently he has been considering the relationship between 'procepts' and imagery.

Effie Maclellan is a senior lecturer in educational studies at the University of Strathclyde. Prior to her move to Strathclyde, she worked for more than 20 years as a class teacher and headteacher in mainstream primary education and special education. Her interest in the mathematical competence and performance of young children continues. Currently, her research focus is on how the primary school mathematics curriculum can best support mathematical conceptualization.

Penny Munn lectures in developmental psychology at the University of Central Lancashire, Preston. Her research interest in the development of literacy and numeracy in the early years began with post-doctoral work on one of Rudolph Schaeffer's projects for Strathclyde Region Education Department and continued with the project described in this book. Her current research examines the implications of these findings for children in the later stages of development.

Ian Sugarman is an advisory teacher for primary mathematics with Shropshire Education Authority, having previously taught in primary schools in Oxfordshire and London. He has been writing curriculum materials for teachers for many years and has devised new items of mathematical equipment, including Route tiles and Diamond tiles. He has contributed articles for several journals, including the NCTM 1992 Yearbook *Calculators in Mathematics Education* and has served on various SCAA committees.

Ian Thompson taught in schools for 19 years before taking up a post in higher education. He currently lectures in mathematics education at the University of Newcastle upon Tyne. Observations of his own young children struggling to make sense of number concepts provided the stimulus for his research into children's idiosyncratic mental calculation strategies. This research later developed into a consideration of personal written algorithms. He feels that it is important that research findings are translated into a form accessible to busy teachers, and to this end publishes frequently in *Child Education* and *The Times Educational Supplement*. He is a member of the Advisory Group for the National Numeracy Project.

Alan Wigley is adviser for mathematics in Wakefield LEA, having previously taught mathematics in secondary schools for 20 years. His main interest is in curriculum developments designed to involve pupils more actively in learning mathematics. He has been involved in projects in both Nottinghamshire and Wakefield, was a co-author of *Journey Into Maths*, and has contributed extensively to publications of the Association of Teachers of Mathematics (ATM). A current interest, the Wakefield Numeracy Initiative, involves the development of a framework of activities for teaching number in primary schools. He is a member of the Advisory Group for the National Numeracy Project.

Editor's preface

This book arose out of my own increasing unease with the structure of the number curriculum for young children as recommended in various official publications and as exemplified in the myriad commercial mathematics schemes on the market. Reading the work of other individuals involved in mathematics education, and gradually realizing that other people were expressing similar or related concerns, provided the final impetus for the appearance of this book.

The book is loosely structured into four sections which deal in turn with: the numerical understanding and beliefs of pre-school children; the place of counting in number development; written number work; and a variety of perspectives on teaching number to young children. These four sections are preceded by a Prologue, which sets the scene for the book, and are then succeeded by an Epilogue, which considers the implications of the views expressed for the teaching of early number.

Most chapters contain cross-references to other parts of the book where specific ideas are dealt with in more detail. Each chapter, however, is self-contained, and is written to be read as a free-standing unit. It is anticipated that the book will be dipped into by readers with an interest in specific aspects of the teaching and learning of early number.

The following information gives details of the ages of children starting school in England and Wales and in Scotland. It is included to help readers who work in a different education system from that operating in Britain.

| School year | | Age on entry |
England and Wales	Scotland	
Reception	Primary 1	4
Year 1 (Y1)	Primary 2	5
Year 2 (Y2)	Primary 3	6
Year 3 (Y3)	Primary 4	7
Year 4 (Y4)	Primary 5	8
Year 5 (Y5)	Primary 6	9
Year 6 (Y6)	Primary 7	10

The early years number curriculum today

Ian Thompson

Introduction

Most commercial mathematics schemes aimed specifically at children in their early years of schooling in Britain tend to be very similar in structure. Those sections concerned with the teaching of early number concepts usually follow a stereotypical sequence. They are likely to contain a substantial collection of activities for children to engage with before they begin to tackle work involving actual numbers. These activities have come to be known as 'pre-number activities', and are considered to be essential prerequisites for basic number work.

While carrying out these activities, children are involved in classifying objects and sorting sets according to different criteria. They partition these sets in a variety of ways (Fig. P. 1), thereby creating mutually exclusive (or disjoint) subsets, and they work with these subsets and their complements. They perform matching activities connecting pictures of identical or related objects, and attempt to find equivalent or non-equivalent sets (Fig. P. 2). They carry out ordering activities which might involve continuing a bead pattern, organizing multilink towers in a sequence according to the number of cubes contained in each tower, or arranging sets in order of size (Fig. P. 3).

Why is it that most early years mathematics schemes appear to maintain such a rigid adherence to this sequence of activities? It seems that there are two main sources of influence which come from two different disciplines: mathematics and psychology. To answer the above question, I shall consider each of these sources of influence separately.

Mathematical developments

By the beginning of the twentieth century, several important developments had taken place in the world of mathematics. New branches of the subject

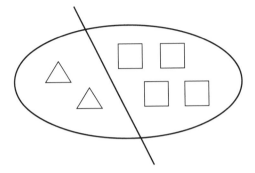

Figure P. 1 Partitioning sets

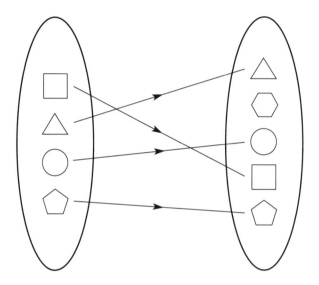

Figure P. 2 Matching sets

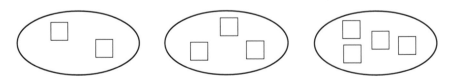

Figure P. 3 Ordering sets

had been developed, and more refined and powerful problem-solving techniques had gradually replaced established standard methods of working. Many traditional areas of mathematics had been re-conceptualized in an attempt to put the subject on a firm logical foundation. In the first half of the century, the influential Bourbaki Group had attempted a systematic description of the myriad mathematical ideas that had been developed over the years. The group was trying to pull together the disparate branches of the subject by emphasizing the major underlying structures and by making use of a more precise and unified language. An important aspect of this unifying language was the terminology which came to be associated in schools with set theory.

The gap between university and school mathematics gradually became wider as the universities responded to the 'mathematical pressure' for change. This widening gap also generated a stimulus for the reforming of the traditional secondary school mathematics curriculum, with the result that the early 1960s saw the emergence in Britain of a variety of 'modern mathematics' projects, such as the Midlands Mathematics Experiment, the Schools Mathematics Project, the Scottish Mathematics Group and various other small-scale projects. Most of these early secondary schemes chose to adopt a fairly rigorous approach to the teaching of the subject.

These innovations took place initially in the elite, academic schools which had the closest ties with the universities; only later did they permeate through to secondary schools in the state sector. Whereas Britain and Denmark responded to these pressures for change by publishing textbooks, other European countries, such as Holland and France, decided to set up commissions.

Inevitably, the fact that changes were taking place in the mathematical diet of secondary age children throughout Europe led to calls for a review of the primary mathematics curriculum. One result of this drive for innovatory activity was the appearance of funded primary projects such as Alef in West Germany, Analogue in France, Wiskobas in Holland and Nuffield in Britain.

The Nuffield Mathematics Project

In 1964, the 'Nuffield Mathematics 5 to 13' Project was launched under the direction of Geoffrey Matthews, a very capable mathematician who had been involved in curriculum development in secondary mathematics, but who was less experienced in the area of primary school teaching. Matthews was very much influenced by the new developments in university mathematics and by the views of the Bourbaki Group in particular. Indeed, an underlying, if not explicit, aim of the Nuffield Project was to ensure that its work was set against the current background of new thinking in higher mathematics. Meetings of the writing team are reported to have been focused more strongly on the mathematical than on the educational aspects of the curriculum development exercise. This interest in mathematical precision and rigour is readily apparent in the approach taken to number in the project, and is clearly illustrated in *Mathematics Begins* (1967), one of the project's earliest publications. This succinct and lucid book contains a rigorous, but eminently readable, account of the important basic ideas underpinning the concept of number. Early sorting activities lead to the development of many of the ideas described earlier, and emphasis is laid on the importance of children gaining substantial experience of these various pre-number concepts before tackling the more complex idea of number. The decision of the project team *not* to produce pupil materials (in retrospect not a wise decision), but to produce teachers' guides instead, led to the departure of some members of the writing team to write their own schemes incorporating pupil booklets.

Harold Fletcher was one such group member, and he later became co-author of the famous – some may say infamous – 'Mathematics for Schools' scheme (or 'Fletcher maths' as it became familiarly known), which was published in 1970. Other schemes began to appear on the market, and finally Nuffield reversed their original decision and launched the Nuffield Mathematics Scheme in 1979. This comprised pupil worksheets and textbooks in addition to the teachers' resource books. Other schemes opted for pupil workbooks instead of worksheets.

Even now, several decades later, there are few commercial mathematics schemes aimed at children in their first years of schooling which do not treat early number in a similar, if not quite so rigorous, manner. Several newly published schemes still reveal the extent to which they, like many other schemes before them, have been influenced by the early Nuffield Project. This influence came from a variety of mainly indirect sources: teachers' centres, university courses, professional association conferences, books on mathematics education and other commercial schemes. Few schemes over the years appear to have questioned the importance, or otherwise, of the accepted approach to early number via specific 'pre-number activities'.

Even though sets, mappings and relations may well be important ideas to take into consideration when undertaking a rigorous analysis of the concept of 'number', it is germane to ask whether these same ideas should necessarily constitute prerequisites for the development of number understanding in young children. Does it automatically follow that ideas which are mathematically sound must also be educationally sound? The following paragraph, which discusses one particular section of the Nuffield book *Computation and Structure: 3* (1968), suggests that the answer to the foregoing question is not necessarily 'yes'.

The booklet explains that the result of adding together two counting numbers is always another counting number, and that a mathematical way of stating this fact is to say that 'the set of counting numbers is closed under the operation of addition'. Unfortunately, however, subtracting two counting numbers does not always generate another counting number. For example, 5 – 7 gives 'negative 2': a number which is not in the set of counting numbers. From a mathematical point of view, subtraction is only closed (i.e. will always give a solution) when the set of integers – which comprise the counting numbers, zero and the negative whole numbers – is involved. Using this extended set of numbers, it is now possible to say that 'the set of integers is closed under the operation of subtraction'. This mathematical nicety led the Nuffield Mathematics Project team (1968) to state that:

Because of the difficulties associated with subtraction in the set {0, 1, 2, 3, ... } it is suggested that the operation, and the techniques for carrying it out, should be deferred until after the introduction of the integers.

This recommendation to delay the teaching of subtraction until children become familiar with negative numbers seems to ignore the wide experience of the 'take-away' aspect of the operation that many young children will have gained in their home environment (see Chapter 2, this volume). Fortunately, this was *not* one of the many ideas adopted by the various textbook writers whose commercial mathematics schemes appeared in the 1970s!

Influences from educational psychology

In the early part of the twentieth century, the predominant theory of learning was behaviourism, with its emphasis on stimulus–response and practice and rewards. However, since the 1960s the theoretical underpinning of much of the thinking about primary mathematics has been the work of Jean Piaget, often regarded as the most influential educational psychologist, but who actually described himself as a 'genetic epistemologist'. His views reflected the climate of the time, in that he attempted to demonstrate that the logical structures associated with set theory were paralleled in children's mental development. The emphasis placed on 'structure' by mathematicians who were Piaget's contemporaries led to his introducing into his developmental theories the idea of a 'grouping' which he had modelled on the mathematical concept of a 'group'.

In reality, Piaget wrote very little about the teaching of mathematics, but nevertheless his theories were to have a profound influence on the thinking of many of those involved in mathematical education. One particular group that found Piaget's theories extremely appealing was the Nuffield Primary Mathematics Project team. So profound was his influence on this group that the project team was to collaborate very closely with him in the early 1970s on the production of assessment materials based on his ingenious clinical tests.

Among the many important ideas contained in his writing, it is probably the concept of conservation that has had the greatest impact on the current approach to teaching early number. Children are said to 'conserve' number if they are aware that when two sets have been shown to be equivalent, either by one-to-one correspondence or by counting, this equivalence is not destroyed by the rearrangement of one of the sets. Piaget (1953) proposed that children generally do not develop this awareness before the age of 6 or 7, and concluded that: 'Children must grasp the principle of conservation of quantity before they can develop the concept of number'.

His emphasis on the importance of conservation led to recommendations by mathematics educators for the delaying of number work until children could conserve number, by which time they would be in a state of 'readiness' for learning. Piaget's research has been replicated on many occasions, and subtle modifications to the tasks have produced results which suggest that young children perform better on these tasks when they make 'human sense' (Donaldson 1978).

Because Piaget's work reflected the scientific context of the first half of the twentieth century, it is easy to see in retrospect why the Nuffield Mathematics Project took the shape that it did. There must have been an irresistible impression of a major convergence between the theories of mathematicians dealing with the foundations of mathematics and the theories of educational psychologists dealing with the modes of thinking of young children.

Conclusion

The authors of the Nuffield Project – influenced by developments in both mathematics and Piagetian psychology – stressed the importance of young children engaging in a variety of pre-number activities involving logical operations before they were exposed to work involving the more difficult concept of abstract number. Underlying this approach was the fundamental belief that there would be transfer of learning from this type of activity to situations involving numbers. One important question to ask is whether there is any evidence to suggest that this transfer actually does take place or that this method of teaching mathematics is superior to others based on different evidence or theories.

In this prologue, I have presented a personal explanation of the reasons for the current structure of the primary mathematics curriculum. At this point one might ask, 'Is there an alternative approach?' . . . (to be continued) . . .

References

Donaldson, M. (1978) *Children's Minds*. London: Fontana.
Nuffield Mathematics Project (1967) *Mathematics Begins*. London: Chambers and Murray.
Nuffield Mathematics Project (1968) *Computation and Structure: 3*. London: Chambers and Murray.
Piaget, J. (1953) How children develop mathematical concepts. *Scientific American*, 189(5): 74–9.

S e c t i o n 1

THE MATHEMATICAL UNDERSTANDING AND BELIEFS OF PRE-SCHOOL CHILDREN

The literature on mathematics education often contains references to 'the mathematics that young children bring with them to school', and occasionally provides anecdotal evidence to illustrate this point. Very few researchers, however, especially in Britain, have attempted to investigate the mathematical knowledge or analyse the level of development of the number understanding of pre-school children. This section of the book contains chapters by two researchers who have been involved in funded projects which have attempted to do just this, and their chapters focus respectively on the beliefs and number understanding of children in nursery and reception classes.

In Chapter 1, Penny Munn argues that the Piagetian orthodoxy of the illogical, egocentric and appearance-led pre-schooler has been challenged by more recent psychological theories which view children as competent individuals managing their social worlds and honing their intellectual skills. In the area of number, there is still a predominant view that children have little understanding of the logic of number. In describing her own research, she builds up a case for arguing that by probing children's subjectivity – ascertaining their own view of the world – we obtain a different view of what seems to be a deficit in logic. Pre-school children appear to have little or no understanding of the adult purpose of counting, which is to find out how many things there are in a collection. The question is raised as to whether the diversity of children's beliefs about counting might account for their apparent numerical incompetence. She argues that early counting is largely an imitative social practice rather than an activity carried out with awareness, and suggests that teachers should assess children's beliefs about counting before involving them in number operations or comparison of quantities; take their counting seriously, as this counting often has a social goal; make the purposes of counting explicit for the children; and stimulate children to develop their own numerical goals, as quantitative counting is often not part of their behavioural repertoire.

In Chapter 2, Carol Aubrey investigates the gap between children's own informal invented number knowledge and the formal requirements of the reception class curriculum. Interviews with reception teachers suggest that commercial schemes have a strong influence on the content and sequence of topics taught, and generally determine when and how addition and subtraction are introduced. Relatively little evidence of children carrying out simple addition and subtraction operations in practical, problem-solving situations was found, despite the fact that over half of the children in her research project had succeeded on four out of five of the addition tasks with concrete representation.

Assessment of children during their first term in reception showed a range of competences in counting, reading and writing numerals, representing quantities and simple addition and subtraction. Those children with the highest rote counting scores tended to have consistently high scores across the range of number tasks. The competences displayed by the children stood in stark contrast to the activities they were being asked to complete. Children did not appear to relate their in-school activities with structured materials to their experience of out-of-school, context-specific problem solving. If new knowledge to be acquired does not appear to have any connection with existing knowledge, children will inevitably have difficulty in establishing new relationships and new understandings.

Children's beliefs about counting

Penny Munn

Introduction

Teachers of young children will be familiar with the traditional view of early number abilities exemplified by the following excerpt:

> One has only to imagine the difficulties of a child who does not understand conservation. Suppose that such a child counts a bowl of oranges and decides that there are six there, and then someone spreads the oranges out into an extended row. If the child thinks that there are more oranges than before, it follows that the child does not really know what the word 'six' really means.
>
> (Nuñes and Bryant 1996: 6)

This example of the traditional view assumes a basic incompetence in children that lies at the heart of any discussion of what children know (or can learn) about number in the infant school. In recent years, developmental psychology has tended to move away from the notion that 'incompetent' children gradually learn to think and act like adults by means of stage-like developments in their cognitive ability. In the 1960s, the discovery of infants' early abilities to make sense of the world and to influence their caregivers led to a revision of assumptions about young children's incompetence. A focus on children's abilities rather than their inabilities led to the emergence of a quite different picture of their development. Studies such as those by Donaldson (1978) and her colleagues illustrated how the very experiments designed to illuminate childish thinking can actually produce incompetence in children. An emphasis on naturalistic observation rather than experiment has shown competent children managing their social worlds and honing their intellectual skills on the daily challenges these worlds present (Richards and Light 1986; Dunn 1988). These changes in developmental psychological theory presented a challenge to the Piagetian orthodoxy of the illogical, egocentric, appearance-led pre-schooler.

Research into children's number knowledge has followed a similar pattern. The belief that young children have no understanding of the nature of number has given way to acknowledgement of early competence. Large research programmes have demonstrated young children's ability to deal with the logic of counting, addition and subtraction. For example, Gelman and Gallistel's (1978) studies have shown that 3- and 4-year-olds recognize the principles of counting provided the quantities that they are dealing with are very small (i.e. no more than 4). Other researchers (e.g. Starkey 1987) have produced results that indicate that very young children use computational procedures.

Despite much research into what children do know about number, the teaching of early number is still constrained by the belief that children have no understanding of the logic of number and that their counting is mere verbalization. Why is this so? The evidence to support such beliefs is easily found by any teacher. Children are unable to conserve number until the age of 6–7 and have problems in applying the 1:1 correspondence principle when they begin to count. We have here a situation in which current research is trying to convey counterintuitive information to practitioners, many of whom, quite sensibly, prefer to believe the evidence of their own eyes.

Currently, researchers are alleging that young children are competent with number, yet simple observation shows that children miss the most obvious implications of number logic until they are older. How is this contradiction to be resolved? In this chapter, I plan to show how a little attention to children's subjectivity – to their own view of the world – casts a wholly different light on what we view as a simple deficit in logic. Anyone's behaviour (whether adult or child) can be misrepresented as illogical if we omit any reference to their personal view, to their beliefs about the world, or to the state of their knowledge. I aim to show that children's behaviour with number can be explained by their beliefs and knowledge about the adult world and that there is no need to hypothesize any inherent deficit in their ability to think and learn.

Instead of reviewing the evidence for the 'deficit' view (far too long a task for a chapter such as this), I shall describe just three sources of evidence for deficits in children's early number logic. The first of these purports to show the lack of organizing principles underlying children's counting activity:

1 Young children may sometimes look very proficient at counting, but their performance breaks down when they're asked to count objects in random arrangements or circles. Under these conditions they usually forget where they began counting and count some objects twice.

The second, number conservation, forms the cornerstone of assumptions that children are not competent with number:

2 When asked to judge the similarity of two rows of objects, children rarely count both rows and compare the results to arrive at their judgement. They judge the rows on their visual properties. Consequently, when one row is squashed up in comparison to the other and the children are asked

whether they are the same or different, they invariably say that the shorter row contains fewer objects.

The third seems to show that children don't really understand the function of counting because they don't use it spontaneously:

3 Three- and 4-year-old children asked to judge the relative quantities in two rows of counters tend to judge by sight. They usually fail to count the rows unless they are specifically prompted to do so by the question 'how many?'.

Considering such overwhelming evidence, how is it possible to assert that young children 'really' have an understanding of number? Note that the three examples rest on observations of *external* aspects of the children's behaviour, with only inferences about their beliefs and knowledge-states. It is the implicit comparison with 'rational' behaviour that creates the picture of a deficit in children's thinking. Our own actions in counting and estimating are automatic and we know immediately what the 'right' response is. It's easy to conclude that small children have a logical deficit that prevents them from seeing the obvious solution.

How can we distance ourselves from such egocentric thinking about children's abilities? Firstly, we can consider number knowledge, not as we experience it in ourselves, but as it develops in young children from around 2 years of age. Secondly, we can include children's subjectivity – their beliefs and knowledge-states – in our accounts of their development. Fuson (1988) has written a very detailed account of the development of number concepts and her broad outline of the early stages is as follows:

Pre-school children
● Children learn to say the number word sequence. Initially, they imitate the string of words. They are also learning the appropriate contexts for counting.
● Children begin to coordinate pointing, objects and number words. They count things as an activity in itself.
● Children integrate counting and cardinality: they begin to use their counting to address questions of 'how many?' when they are asked this question.

School-age children
● Children begin to count from any point in the chain, not just the beginning (one, two, etc.). This allows 'counting on' strategies to develop.
● Number words in themselves become countable items for children. This gives them a flexible means of solving addition and subtraction.

For pre-schoolers, in particular, this is not a *single* development in number understanding, but multiple overlapping developments in verbal, motor and cognitive activities that become integrated with each other over time. We know very clearly, then, how children's *actions* with number change over time. How do their beliefs change and what is the relation between their actions and their beliefs?

Counting

I shall use the framework of the pre-school number development that Fuson (1988) has outlined to describe some changes in pre-schoolers' counting and beliefs about counting. The data come from a study of Scottish children I followed through the final year of nursery and into the first term of primary school. The children were 51 months old on average when I first visited them in nursery and were 64 months old on average at the final visit, when they were in Primary 1. They attended eight nurseries in the Glasgow area and comprised twenty-five girls and thirty-one boys, all but one having English as their first language. I talked to them individually about number and reading at each of four visits, asking them whether they could count and read, and playing a series of games designed to illuminate their understanding of number (see Munn 1994). The main points of the interview were:

1 'Can you count?' – this elicited each child's number word sequence independent of an object count.
2 'Can you count these blocks?' (maximum of 36) – this elicited an object count.
3 'Could you give me (one, two, three, etc.) blocks?' – this elicited each child's cardinal number concepts.
4 'Do you count at home? What do you count? Why do you count?' – these questions elicited a description of the children's understanding of counting and of their beliefs about this activity.

Over the four visits, the children's responses changed in a coherent and systematic manner. Their ability to recite the number sequence was usually in advance of their ability to give or to count blocks. Their number recitation showed a distinct pattern of development. First, they memorized the number words to ten. Then after a little time they memorized the number words to twenty or twenty-nine. Much later they began to generate the number sequence between thirty and fifty or sixty. They remembered the ordering of the 'ty' words and used the nine before thirty, forty, etc., as a cue to generate the next number word ending in 'ty'. During this time they became more competent at coordinating word and gesture (pointing to the blocks while counting) and their cardinal number concepts (ability to 'give a number') gradually extended.

Below are the responses of three of the children with good counting skills – Andrew, Roger and Alison – at each of the interviews. Each child's age in months (denoted by 'm') at each interview is given on the left. The first datum is the last correct word of the child's number word recitation. The second datum is the last correctly pointed number word of the child's count and point routine. The third and final datum is the child's last correctly given quantity. The three children's data demonstrate the very slow progression in cardinal number concepts and the way that these trailed behind verbal counting.

Andrew
[visit 1, 47 m]: Counts to 19, counts 20 blocks, gives 4 blocks
[visit 2, 52 m]: Counts to 29, counts 29 blocks, gives 9 blocks
[visit 3, 55 m]: Counts to 29, counts 32 blocks, gives 7 blocks
[visit 4, 60 m]: Counts to 39, counts 34 blocks, gives 10 blocks

Roger
[visit 1, 53 m]: Counts to 14, counts 14 blocks, gives 4 blocks
[visit 2, 58 m]: Counts to 49, counts 19 blocks, gives 10 blocks
[visit 3, 61 m]: Counts to nearly 100, counts 36 blocks, gives 7 blocks
[visit 4, 66 m]: Counts to over 100, counts 35 blocks, gives 6 blocks

Alison
[visit 1, 51 m]: Counts to 5, counts 5 blocks, gives 3 blocks
[visit 2, 46 m]: Counts to 10, counts 5 blocks, gives 4 blocks
[visit 3, 54 m]: Counts to 14, counts 6 blocks, gives 6 blocks
[visit 4, 59 m]: Counts to 14, counts 14 blocks, gives 10 blocks

Beliefs about counting

The children's responses to the questions 'What do you count?' and 'Why do you count?' showed that it was very rare for them to understand the adult purpose of counting before they went to school. After school entry, some children seemed to have gained a little understanding, but it was uncommon to have a child respond to the 'Why?' question by saying 'To know how many'. This was true even for those children who were quite competent at the counting involved in giving nine or ten blocks. They could count in all three senses: saying the words, linking the words with the objects, and linking the last word in the sequence with the amount. Yet only one of the children at the pre-school visits responded to the 'Why?' question by replying 'To know the many'. The rest of the children showed by their responses that they were perplexed by the notion of counting as a purposeful activity. One little girl at the first visit (age 48 months) responded to the question 'What do you count at home?' by saying, 'But counting's just saying the words, isn't it?'.

Despite the nature of the children's beliefs about counting, they all said that they *could* count, showing that they believed that to count was to say the words in the correct order. It was only at the visit after school entry (average age 64 months) that some of the children began to say confidently that they counted 'to know how many things they had'. They also began to quote contexts in which they themselves might want to tally objects (in the following, C = child, I = interviewer):

C: My Mum's pennies – just her pennies.
I: Why does she count her pennies?
C: Because she needs to know how many she needs to buy things.

I: Anything else that you count when you are at home?

C: Just my teddies and my pens.

I: Why do you count your teddies and your pens?

C: To see how many I have got so that I know how many colours I need.

Not all the children were this sophisticated on school entry. There were three categories of reply to the 'what' question and four categories of reply to the 'why' question. When asked *why* they counted at home, children gave answers that fell into one of the following four categories (apart from 'uncodeable' responses, such as conversation switches and obscure reference):

Category 1: Counting to please the self
These responses contained reasons not really connected with counting, or simple assertions of desires:

Because I want to.
Cos I do.
So people can sit in them [i.e. the chairs that this child counted].

Category 2: Counting to conform to others' expectations
This group of responses contained reasons that were related to other people's desires for their activity:

My cousin tells me to.
Because my mummy and daddy want me to.

Category 3: Counting in order to learn
This group of responses contained explicit references to learning:

Cos so I can know my numbers.
To learn all my numbers.

Category 4: Counting to know how many there are
It was only this type of response that contained any direct reference to quantification, to knowing how many things there were once one had counted:

To know how many toys there are.

Five of the children gave category 4 responses as a reason for counting. Seven of the children gave category 3 responses and two of the children gave category 2 responses. The remainder were either uncodeable or gave category 1 responses. This distribution of responses suggests that it takes children quite a long time to grow out of the stage of counting as an activity in itself. Those children who said they counted to learn seemed to be very aware of the role that numbers and counting played in school. They still saw the activity of counting as an end in itself, but as a school activity rather than the play activity it had previously been.

After they had started school, the children were more willing to answer the question 'what do you count', but the variety of responses indicated that children still held beliefs about counting that were at variance with adult beliefs about counting as verbal quantification. Children's responses to the question 'What do you count?' fell into three categories:

Category 1: Counting as a verbal activity
These responses indicated that counting was still seen as an activity in itself:

To forty.
To ten.
One, two, three, four, five, six, seven, eight, nine, ten, eleven, twelve, thirteen, fourteen, fifteen, sixteen, seventeen, eighteen, nineteen, twenty.

Category 2: Counting as an object-related activity
These responses showed an interpretation of the question that was quite consistent with a notion of counting as quantification:

Stones.
Trees.
Dollies.
My toys.

Category 3: Counting as reading and writing numerals
These responses cited reading or writing numerals as examples of 'counting':

Numbers on the fridge.
I have got this book and it has got numbers in it, and she [sister] always tells me it. She tells me a high number.

After school entry, only three children still gave only category 1 responses to the question 'What do you count?'. There were, then, very few children who clung to the pre-school definition of counting as a purely verbal activity existing just for itself. Twenty-seven of the children gave category 2 responses. However, eleven of these mixed this with a response from the first category, indicating that they still thought of counting as a playful activity. Five children mixed category 2 responses with category 3 responses, indicating that they associated counting with reading and writing numbers. This pattern of responses showed that even after the development of object-related counting, the children still retained some earlier associations. The activity of 'counting' was associated with the purely verbal activity of their infancy, with the writing and reading of numerals that they did with other family members, or with the learning that they knew was part and parcel of school activity.

Why was it that these children, who could count and who had number concepts, had such diverse beliefs about the purpose of counting? There is no single feature of their thinking that will explain this. Pre-school children's understanding of other people's mental activity is still very undeveloped. Children's experience of counting games with adults is often simply playful. Often in joint counting the quantitative goal is absent or is not made explicit. This, together with young children's natural focus on physical action rather than mental aspects of activity, serves to obscure the adult function of counting from them for rather a long time. Children are also dependent on adults for most things and for this reason they have no real need to tally objects, keep score or keep count. Quite the opposite – count words are more likely to have a playful purpose, to be part of a game such as hide and seek, or a playful routine with adults or older children. Games of 'how high can I count' or routines embedded in daily life, such as ritual counting of steps or other landmarks, very rarely have purposeful counting as a central feature.

The diversity of children's beliefs about counting can in itself account for their apparent numerical incompetence – their tendency to count on past the beginning of a circle of objects, to speak as though items change in number when the shape of an array changes, their failure to count spontaneously to solve a quantitative problem. These features of children's lives, and the beliefs consequent on them, may be sufficient in themselves to explain the nature of young children's engagement with the number system. Once children begin to develop quantitative numerical goals for themselves, they will start to generate the logical properties that we automatically associate with number.

Discussion

There were very clear differences between the pre-school children's actions on the one hand and their beliefs on the other. Although the children's counting ability was often extensive and accurate, they had remarkably little sense of the adult definition of counting as they went to school. They seemed to believe that counting had a playful purpose and they didn't really connect it with quantification. The progression outlined here demonstrates the influence that social beliefs can have on cognitive development. There was a clear disjunction between the children's counting behaviour and their beliefs about counting. This indicates that, although the children may implicitly follow some of the principles of counting, early counting is essentially an imitative social practice rather than an activity done with awareness. The point at which their activity began to change from social practice to self-aware cognitive activity was a point of social transition. For some of the children it was school entry that seemed to trigger this change in beliefs about counting, a transition that causes both changes in experience and a transformation in identity. This gives us reason to suppose that the changes in the children – these progressions in belief – were related to changes in their social environment.

Implications for teaching

The approach outlined here contrasts strongly with existing interventions, in which researchers have devised quite complicated methods for training children to count (see, for example, Cowan *et al.* 1993). Rather than providing positive reinforcement for counting, this approach rests on the understanding that children's beliefs are central to their development. The suggested intervention nominates four activities to lead young children into counting: monitoring beliefs, taking children's counting seriously, talking about goals when counting and stimulating the development of children's numerical goals. The aim is to manipulate children's beliefs so that they are naturally led towards the goal of counting.

1   *Assess children's beliefs about counting before working on addition, subtraction or comparison of quantities.* One of the main features of young children's behaviour with number is that they don't count where it would be useful for them to do so. The argument presented in this chapter is that this is related to their belief that counting is playful rather than quantitative. Since any sort of comparison, addition or subtraction will involve counting, it makes sense to check whether children believe there is a relation between counting and quantification before commencing any activities with a numerical goal. If children don't have this belief then the activity's presentation can be modified accordingly.

2   *Take young children's counting seriously.* Counting without quantification is not necessarily meaningless, and is certainly not meaningless to small children. The purely verbal counting seen in young children has received particularly bad publicity because it has been seen as a trap for the unwary teacher who might otherwise attribute far too much number-knowledge to young children. However, it would do very little harm to loosen the criterion for what counts as using number. Young children's counting often has a social rather than a numerical goal. For instance, children may recite the number sequence to imitate an admired family member, to show that they can count or to take part in a well-established ritual. It is important not to negate non-numerical counting, as it can provide a point of contact with a child's social being. Adults also have count sequences with a purely social goal. Take, for example, the teacher who says, 'I want quiet please! One, two three four, five!' This is every bit as much a social and ritual use of the number sequence as the young child's counting. So, too, is much of the adult's counting that takes place in the home as a means of informal teaching. Such counting provides a framework for the development of properly numerical counting and as such it should be gently encouraged. Conversations with children about 'big' numbers also have a social rather than a purely numerical goal. As with counting, these should be encouraged.

3   *Make the purpose of counting explicit for children.* We often assume that our purposes and goals are clear to others – so much so that it is often a surprise to discover that children don't understand why we are doing quite simple things. If activities with counting are presented in contexts where adult goals can be mused on out loud, then children will have more chance of grasping the mental aspect of the activity that they see. One of the

strengths of 'Sesame Street' is the extent to which the characters 'think out loud' in everyday contexts, providing children with explicit knowledge of other people's goals.

4 *Stimulate children to develop their own numerical goals*. Much of young children's failure to count is related to the lack of numerical goals embedded in their lives. They rarely form an intention to check, tally to enumerate or compare, and so quantitative counting simply does not form part of their behavioural repertoire. As children mature, they may adopt some of their parents' goals – particularly in relation to money – or they may develop goals of their own related to sharing or to getting things just right. A numerical agenda that comes from the child's own life will be a more powerful stimulator of counting than any adult-imposed goal. One little boy told me that he usually counted his yoghurts when he got home, because his mother always pretended she had eaten some while he was at school. This was much more effective as a number lesson than helping to lay the table. It illustrates the difference between imposing an adult numerical goal and helping children to develop their own numerical goals.

Conclusions

Children's number abilities are puzzlingly slow to develop into full adult form. Even the most basic number skill of counting takes some years to develop. It is not until children acquire some experience of the mental activity involved in other people's counting that they are able to adopt these elementary number activities completely. They begin their learning by imitating the external appearance of number activities and only gradually adopt the goals that adults and older children have when they engage in such activity. Once they understand the mental aspects of the activities they see others doing, then they are able to copy the goal of an action as well as its external appearance. The data from the Scottish pre-school study broadly support Vygotskian notions of how development proceeds. First, counting appears on the social plane, between people, with children's activity supported by adult language and goals. After considerable experience of this joint action, children internalize the cultural practice of counting. It then appears on the psychological plane, at which point children are able to direct their counting according to adult principles.

The direction that development takes – whether from practice to principles or principles to practice – has very important implications for the early maths curriculum. If the direction is from principles to practice – that is, children first understand the principles of counting and then develop counting ability – then the current assumptions about early maths are entirely valid. If ability develops out of principled knowledge, then it is entirely sensible to suppress all counting and all talk of large numbers until children properly understand both counting and numbers (around age 6–7 years). If, on the other hand, the practice itself is important, then it follows that sheer amount of experience – whether understood or not – will in itself aid development.

There has been some argument about the causal, underpinning of number development – whether practice leads to principle or vice versa (for a discussion, see Nuñes and Bryant 1996: 25–6). It is important to note that we require experimental evidence to decide this question definitely. The correlational data that were drawn from the Scottish pre-school study do not permit us to infer cause; some other factor, such as language ability, may have been affecting both measures. However, the data do seem to indicate that experience with counting is unlikely to hinder children in their number understanding, however lacking in logic their behaviour might appear to be. This brings us back to my main argument, which is that young children's interactions with number are made to appear illogical by distancing them from their context of subjective awareness and belief. Once this context is sketched in, however briefly, then it becomes easier to adopt a 'whole child' approach with respect to number.

Acknowledgements

This study was supported by ESRC Grant L208252005 and was part of the ESRC programme 'Innovation and Change in Education'. Thanks are due to the pre-school centres who took part in the study and to Strathclyde Region Education Department for help and cooperation.

References

Cowan, R., Foster, C.M. and Al-Zubaidi, A.S. (1993) Encouraging children to count. *British Journal of Developmental Psychology*, 11: 411–20.
Donaldson, M. (1978) *Children's Minds*. London: Fontana.
Dunn, J. (1988) *The Beginnings of Social Understanding*. Oxford: Blackwell.
Fuson, K.C. (1988) *Children's Counting and Concepts of Number*. New York: Springer-Verlag.
Gelman, R. and Gallistel, C.R. (1978) *The Child's Understanding of Number*. Cambridge, MA: Harvard University Press.
Munn, P. (1994) The early development of literacy and numeracy skills. *European Early Childhood Education Research Journal*, 2(1): 5–18.
Nuñes, T. and Bryant, P. (1996) *Children Doing Mathematics*. Oxford: Blackwell.
Richards, M. and Light, P. (eds) (1986) *Children of Social Worlds*. Oxford: Blackwell.
Starkey, P. (1987) *Early arithmetic competencies*. Paper presented at the biennial meeting of the Society for Research in Child Development. Baltimore, MD, April.

Children's early learning of number in school and out

Carol Aubrey

Background and introduction

There is strong empirical evidence to support the view that formal schooling and the type of cognitive activity that it stimulates lacks continuity with the rich, practical knowledge required for informal problem-solving of everyday social contexts. Lave (1988) has shown how arithmetic of the real world does not reflect the formal procedures taught in the classroom. Nuñes *et al.* (1993) have suggested that young Brazilian street traders, for instance, display a situated construction of arithmetic knowledge in their invented methods of calculation, which is almost without errors. This competence, however, does *not* translate to classroom contexts.

Clearly, classroom teachers and pupils are also engaged in everyday, situated activity of a kind but how, and to what extent, can this activity be applied to the world outside? On the one hand, repeated reform of the school curriculum has led to changes in the relationship of in-school arithmetic to ordinary, everyday life and, on the other hand, society itself has also changed and with it the requirements for social competence. In terms of the school curriculum, formally taught procedures for calculation, measurement and handling of money have been generated and institutionalized in a formal problem-solving which bears little resemblance to the world children experience outside school. The consequence of this may be that children, themselves, do not associate their informally acquired knowledge about number with the rules, properties and procedures of school arithmetic. But, if formal school arithmetic does *not* contribute to everyday, out-of-school number competence and, vice versa, is this something which the reception teacher should be more aware of? Can or should this informal knowledge acquired before schooling begins be used to support in-school learning? This chapter will investigate the gap between children's own informal, invented number knowledge and the formal requirements of the reception class curriculum by drawing on findings from an on-going project at the University of Durham (Aubrey 1997). This will lead to consideration of the role such knowledge *could* have in the planning of reception class teaching.

The development of early, out-of-school number skills

From the first weeks of life, human infants appear to have a fundamental sense of quantity. This is demonstrated in their response to numerical features presented to them and suggests a capacity to represent mentally quantities of up to four. By 18 months, moreover, infants seem to recognize and respond to ordinal relationships; that is, they recognize that three items is more than two items or vice versa.

During the years before school, children learn number words, begin to relate number language to their existing number sense, as well as develop an appreciation of the ways that these number words can be used for counting and measurement (Fuson 1988). Over this period, children extend this knowledge from smaller to larger quantities and apply it to an increasing range of activities and social contexts in the course of which number-based strategies become increasingly differentiated from early perception-based strategies, that is, subitizing, or instant recognition of small groups of items.

Early intuitive knowledge of arithmetic of infants for very small quantities (e.g. 1 + 1) and of young, pre-school children (e.g. 3 − 1) gradually increases alongside the development and deployment of counting skills (Fuson 1988). Growing appreciation that addition increases and subtraction decreases quantity is supported by the use of fingers to support counting and is reinforced by early parent–child and pre-school, number-based songs, rhymes and activities.

To solve simple problems, however, children need not only sound knowledge of number, counting and basic arithmetic, but comprehension of relationship statements, such as 'more', 'less' or 'different', their representation and their translation into particular arithmetic operations. As children move beyond representing these operations fully with the items involved, from fingers or manipulatives to derived fact strategies, increasingly problem-solving comprehension, working memory and basic computation skills are involved (Geary 1994).

It appears that in all cultures where addition and subtraction problems are common, children draw on their existing understanding of number, quantity and arithmetic upon which knowledge of the counting system has been based to develop a range of strategies (Carpenter and Moser 1982).

If early arithmetic *is* universal, as appears to be the case, then clearly the most powerful influence on arithmetic development is formal schooling. This provides the strongest argument for the reception teacher's understanding of children's intuitive knowledge of number and early arithmetic problem-solving of addition and subtraction, with its early recognition of quantity shifting to finger counting and, later, to verbal counting and fact retrieval.

This brief overview serves to underline the central importance of linking young children's existing arithmetic and problem-solving skills carefully to in-school arithmetic and institutionalized systems, routines and representations of school number work, and reveals the complexity of the reception teacher's task.

The nature of reception class mathematics

Conventionally, the UK infant curriculum has attempted to develop mathematical thinking and ideas through activities which allow the handling, comparing and ordering of objects derived from Piaget and theory of sets, relations and mapping, exemplified in early curriculum projects of the 1960s and still reflected in infant scheme work (see Prologue, this volume). More recently, this has been overlaid with content reflecting the mathematics National Curriculum, which includes number, algebra, shape and space and handling data.

Various stages of the Durham Project, which included interviews and observation, have attempted to shed light on current reception practice. In interview, reception teachers reported using a topic-based approach to curriculum planning into which early number work was incorporated. The topic 'Ourselves', for instance, provided the opportunity to design tasks which allowed non-standard measurement with body parts, comparison and difference, the preparation of simple graphs, charts of heights, lengths and sizes, the introduction of simple concepts of time, consideration of house numbers, and the use of sets of eye and hair colour to introduce simple mapping. At the same time, the provision of practical work and the freedom to choose were regarded as important, since the reception class was believed to be 'extended nursery'. Mathematical language was seen to arise naturally from play, games, stories, songs and jingles, from sand, water and construction play, as well as from card and board games and 'shop' play. Through these activities, pattern for algebra and data handling, language of measurement and position, comparison and difference, all would be introduced.

It was recognized from both nursery records and from teachers' own simple assessment that some children entered school knowing colours and counting, showing shape recognition and measurement language, and it was felt that this knowledge should be extended through sorting and matching by shape, size and colour, data handling, using pets and favourite foods, construction and copying 2D and 3D shapes. In number, counting, matching and recording would be practised through worksheet material, as well as through computer, card and board number games. Once one-to-one correspondence was established, the children would learn number concepts one to six, then one to ten, as well as zero.

From discussion with teachers, it appeared that formal infant mathematics scheme work was a strong influence on the content and sequence of topics taught. In fact, all teachers reported use of published scheme material, although the point at which this was introduced varied from the first month of schooling for one teacher, to Easter time of the reception year for another and, in yet another case, it was left until the children's second year of schooling. Scheme material was used in a variety of ways and for a variety of purposes. It was seen to run alongside and to be reinforced by practical work as well as to provide a basis for assessment. It was thought to offer a framework for planning the introduction of sorting, matching and ordering numbers. More significantly, scheme work *determined* when and how addition and subtraction were introduced. The introduction of addition and subtraction was described in terms of reaching the relevant book of the scheme concerned, whether this was the Scottish Primary Mathematics (SPMG) or Cambridge Infant Mathematics (IMP), though this would take place in conjunction with apparatus and practical activity and would lead eventually to representation and formal recording (Aubrey 1997).

Subsequent observation of different reception classes over different phases of the project have confirmed teachers' reported practice with much emphasis placed on practical colour, pattern and shape recognition, matching, sorting and ordering of shape, comparison and ordering of quantity, counting and recording and comparison of sets. There was evidence of the influence of scheme work in the presentation of tasks, the orderly introduction of numbers one to six, and zero to ten, with reading, tracing, copying and writing numerals, matching and sorting of corresponding sets of objects. This activity was reinforced with songs, jingles and games. Significantly, there was relatively little evidence of children carrying out simple addition and subtraction operations in practical, problem-solving situations. In one phase of the project, which followed seven teachers through the reception year, three of eighteen lessons observed involved these operations for one teacher, two of nineteen for another, one out of twenty for yet another, and none for a further four reception class teachers.

What reception-aged children actually knew at school entry

To establish exactly what mathematical knowledge children brought into school, the early phases of the project investigated the informal mathematical knowledge displayed by young children before formal instruction began. The Durham Project started at exactly the same time as the National Curriculum was introduced for 5- to 7-year-olds and, while reception-aged children were not officially included, it was assumed that this might have an impact on the curriculum for 4- to 5-year-olds. Assessment of children's number knowledge was thus designed to reflect the range of numerical competences that develop in the pre-school years in ways which were, at the same time, compatible with key content of the National Curriculum for mathematics at its first level. This served to give ecological validity to the assessment situation.

Assessment tasks were constructed in the form of long, practical assessment interviews with individual children. Tasks involved everyday objects and activities already familiar to the children, in the hope that they would

actively construct meaning with the interviewer, and hence offer an indication of their current level of knowledge and skills, their strategies and forms
of representation. All assessment took place in the first half of the children's
first term in school so as to document informal knowledge acquired in out-
of-school contexts rather than in-school procedures.

Assessment of the prior knowledge actually brought into school by forty-
eight children of the interviewed teachers and confirmed by a further group
of sixty-seven children from a variety of social backgrounds showed a range
of competences in counting, recognition of numerals, representation of quantities, simple addition and subtraction, social sharing and simple multiplication by continuous addition, as well as appropriate language for comparing
and ordering objects for position in space and on a line, and for selecting
criteria appropriately to sort objects.

To access children's counting words, they were asked to see how far they
could count for a Panda puppet. The highest number achieved on two trials
without violating the conventional number order was taken as a measure of
the child's rote counting. Counting ranged from four to more than 100, with
a mean length of sixteen, with 80 per cent of children counting to at least
ten, 48 per cent of children counting to within the range eleven to twenty,
and a further 15 per cent to within the range twenty-one to thirty.

A similar number of children (81 per cent) were able to carry out an order
invariance task, counting from the beginning, end and middle of a small
array of toys. The purpose of this task was to assess children's understanding
that arrays of objects counted in a different order yield the same value.

Reading numbers showed variable performance, with 50 per cent of children recognizing five to nine or more numbers, a further 31 per cent recognizing two to four numbers, and 19 per cent recognizing none or one number.
The purpose here was to assess children's ability to recognize written numerals
by presenting everyday objects or people bearing the numbers 1 to 10, 12,
15 and 27.

Writing numbers again showed variable performance, from those knowing
no numbers at all to those knowing all the numbers presented (1–10, 12, 15
and 21), and in fact some 50 per cent knew at least five numbers. All children, however, could represent on paper different quantities of bricks, using
tallies, squiggles or other simple symbols.

Counting on forwards from a given number for the Panda puppet showed,
again, variable performance for a task intended to indicate whether or not
children were beginning to develop more abstract and flexible counting
strategies. Twenty-five per cent of children counted on forwards one number
for between four to seven randomly presented numbers, 27 per cent managed one to three numbers, and 35.5 per cent managed eight to ten numbers. Only 12.5 per cent of children could not manage this task.

For counting backwards from a given number, 17 per cent of children were
able to count backwards for eight to ten randomly presented numbers, 15
per cent of children were able to count backwards for four to seven numbers,
50 per cent counted backwards for only one to three numbers and 19 per
cent counted backwards for none of the presented numbers.

For understanding of the number operations addition and subtraction, the children were given the very simplest 'join' and 'separate' problems with concrete materials. The children were told, for instance, 'Panda wants to buy some ice cream. We give him three pennies'. (Three pennies from a pile were placed in front of the child.) 'Now he says that he really wants *four* pennies. Can you fix it so that he gets four pennies?'

For addition with concrete representation, involving the glove puppet in simple addition with small numbers of coins (within 10), 51 per cent of children gained a score of 4 or 5 out of 5 for addition, 39 per cent scored 1–3 and 10 per cent scored nil. For a similar task of subtraction with concrete representation, again using the puppet and coins to represent the operation, 63 per cent of children scored 4 or 5 out of 5, a further 24 per cent scored between 1 and 3 and 13 per cent scored nil.

For a simple division by social sharing task, 73 per cent of children scored 4 or 5 out of 5 on tasks calling for simple distribution of sweets among two and three bears, 25 per cent scored 1–3 and 2 per cent scored nil. For multiplication by simple addition, 66 per cent were able to carry out two simple tasks checking children's understanding of a small set being repeated, 13 per cent scored 1 and 21 per cent scored nil.

Most challenging was the diversity of knowledge, skills and strategies in a variety of number, counting and arithmetic tasks within the group. The children with highest rote counting scores tended to have consistently high scores across number tasks and were well towards mastery of the first level of the National Curriculum. Other children with particularly low scores for rote counting were able to manage tasks with small numbers only and showed less stable counting procedures, with inaccuracy increasing with the size of the number.

As other studies have shown, the children from the lower socio-economic groups had lower entry scores but, in a subsequent phase of the project which re-assessed the children at the end of the reception year, they were shown to have made significant progress. The largest number to which the children could correctly count increased from a mean of 14.7 to 43, with a range of 8–29. In the reading numbers activity, the largest number recognized increased from a mean of 4.8 to 9.7, with a range of 0–10, and writing numbers increased from a mean of 3 written numbers to a mean of 10. Counting on forwards increased from a mean of 6 numbers to a mean of 9.1 numbers and counting backwards from a mean of 2.7 to 7.9. Addition increased from a mean of 3 to 4.8 out of 5. For subtraction, most children scored highly on school entry and thus there were no significant changes.

The range and diversity of competences displayed by these young children at school entry, as well as the nature and direction of infants' and young children's development of arithmetic skills, stands in contrast to the traditional reception curriculum and infant scheme content which, as noted earlier, follows a sequence of sorting, matching and classifying, joining and separating of sets, counting and ordering, recognizing and writing numbers 0 to 10, where simple mathematical relationships are represented with concrete materials, and topics such as measurement and shape run alongside.

The implications for teaching and learning

Returning to the initial distinction made between in-school and out-of-school mathematics, observations of practice suggest that the school-learned arithmetic curriculum may not support and develop the flexible use of children's existing, informal strategies. Arithmetic used in out-of-school settings is represented by the objects being manipulated. The reception class conventions which emphasize set theory and the representation of numbers in structured number apparatus may bear little relationship to real problem-solving outside school and may not be easily translated to solve problems outside the classroom context or connected to out-of-school knowledge embedded in out-of-school contexts. The variety of forms of representing numerical ideas used in the classroom may appear to provide children with the means for better understanding though, interestingly, research findings in this area are mixed. To take one example, while it is well-established that many young children solve addition and subtraction word problems, using counting strategies and manipulating relevant materials, and the results of the project assessment showed these reception-aged children could do this, there were very few examples of teachers introducing such problems in the children's reception year.

What is most likely to occur is that children do not relate their classroom interactions with the associated use of structured materials to their existing out-of-school problem-solving. In other words, they interpret the materials in terms of the classroom tasks provided but do not recognize any match between these activities, the supposed underlying numerical relationships, and the real world of problem-solving outside school. The work carried out on sets, for instance, is likely to be very far removed from children's existing knowledge, the representations with which they are familiar, and the social contexts in which they are used. Few cues supporting such connections appear to be made in the classroom, leaving a contextual distance between in-school and out-of-school mathematics.

Another aspect is the relation between the materials used for manipulation and the social situation in which the materials are used. A question which springs to mind is: Does the activity being carried out help to gain attention and focus *shared* experience? Teacher–child communication could have been enhanced by emphasizing relevant relationships of classroom activities to children's existing experience. In other words, the social context in which materials are being used in the classroom and the discussion generated *may* account for their ineffectiveness in increasing children's understanding. Other questions to ask are: Are the representation systems being used connected to children's existing network of knowledge? Concrete materials provide a representation which can be linked to children's existing experience. In fact, the reception class curriculum may easily serve to provide isolated information unconnected to existing networks, which places a correspondingly high load on memory for the child and does not promote transfer. The kind of work presented to children influences how they think about the subject and what they believe about its nature. If they are asked to carry out meaningless procedures and rules for manipulating materials as isolated information, they will believe mathematics involves the learning of narrow concepts and rigid rules. Significantly, subsequent interviews with the project reception teachers revealed that although they believed in the value of practical activity, their own experience of learning mathematics in primary schools had been of a narrow and procedural kind.

In summary, arithmetic used out of school is represented fully with physical objects related to the problem. In contrast, school mathematics is represented in a new vocabulary, new activities and operations and new apparatus, and often little explicit teaching of the relationships of this to children's existing knowledge is carried out. Children *should* be able to interpret new situations in terms of what is already known. If new knowledge appears to have little relationship to existing knowledge and ideas, it will be difficult for new relationships to be established and new understanding to be gained. Even if analogies and alternative representations are used, then their effectiveness is in direct relation to connections made to existing knowledge. As has been shown, children have extensive informal knowledge which they can apply to everyday situations. This provides a potential starting point for teaching based on children's existing knowledge, though of course it does not suggest *how* that knowledge can be integrated with developing networks of knowledge and procedures of in-school mathematics. Procedures and concepts cannot, however, be taught as isolated bits of information.

The first point to consider, then, is: What existing knowledge do children have and how can this be extended? A 'bottom-up' model of instruction will reflect children's existing thinking, and teaching which emphasizes connections made between prior problem-solving and new mathematical concepts and procedures. While UK curriculum reforms of the 1980s have emphasized analysis of mathematical knowledge and content, curriculum innovation in other parts of the world has emphasized the use of problem contexts to develop meaning and situations that have relevance for pupils. In the United States, for instance, Carpenter *et al.* (1989) have argued for a better appreciation and use to be made of children's informal knowledge in school instruction. Their argument rests on four related assumptions underlying recent research into children's learning:

- children construct their own mathematical knowledge;
- mathematics should be organized to facilitate children's construction of their knowledge;
- children's development of mathematical ideas should provide the basis for sequencing topics for instruction;
- mathematical skills should be taught in relation to understanding and problem-solving.

These assumptions emphasize the importance of meaningful learning of mathematics through modifying and building on existing knowledge and thinking. By providing their first-grade teachers (for 6-year-olds) with a structure and analysis of children's own developing competence in arithmetical problem-solving – in particular, with knowledge about the types of addition and subtraction problems and the strategies children typically used to solve problems – they found that the teachers were able to use this knowledge in their teaching. This provided them with an effective means to evaluate how their *existing* curriculum fitted to the children's own problem-solving skills. It also offered a sequence for instruction and resulted in gains in children's solving of complicated classroom problem-solving as well as skills in basic arithmetic. Moreover, the teachers were more likely to attend to their children's solution strategies.

Kamii (1989) also allowed children in first- and second-grade classrooms (for 6- and 7-year-olds) to 'reinvent arithmetic' through social interaction stimulated by mathematical games. This led to striking differences in explanations offered by children for the solutions they obtained, as well as higher attainment on standard tests and understanding of place value by the 7-year-olds.

French 'didactical theory' has also assumed that children must actively interpret and make sense of their classroom experience and that their knowledge is derived from problems encountered in everyday life. French researchers, according to Balacheff (1990), collaborated with class teachers to design problem-solving activities which called for children to act upon and evaluate their constructions of knowledge through classroom discussion. Similar work has been found effective in the United States by Cobb (1988) and in South Africa by Murray *et al.* (1993).

Dutch realistic primary mathematics teaching has avoided entirely the introduction of set theory and stresses rich thematic and concrete contexts, integration of mathematics with other subjects, differentiated individual learning processes and working together in heterogeneous groups. Concrete materials are regarded as an aid only to solve certain problems. Teaching of addition and subtraction to 6-year-olds, for instance, is built round 'The Bus' (*Wiskobas*). Young children play mathematical drama and illustrative scenes of getting on and off a bus. Sums are then presented in drawings of buses linked by arrows which indicate the direction and carry a sign showing how many people got on or off the bus. The number is written on the side and the bus is faded as meaning is established. Children's own invented strategies are encouraged and even incorrect solutions valued as a means to consider practical problem-solving in specific contexts. Again the approach has been associated with significant differences in the time taken to learn arithmetic.

Analysis of numerical understanding, however, does not stop at children's existing competence, but leads to the consideration of how well teachers' *own* knowledge is connected to this. Parallels may be drawn between the way teachers, themselves, were taught and the teaching they implement. As noted above, findings from the Durham Project suggest that teachers' intuitive knowledge about children and teaching may *not* be well-connected to this analysis of children's existing knowledge. Teachers themselves, in interview, described their own primary teaching experiences where they had worked largely alone in classrooms to memorize rules and narrow concepts. This knowledge is in contrast to the rich, informal knowledge acquired in out-of-school settings observed to be brought into school by their pupils.

Conclusions

Research on the development of children's early number skills provides a basis for analysing the existing curriculum and a set of principles for relating children's strategies to this. Teaching which focuses on fine-grained analysis of the way teaching and learning interacts will contribute to the development of teachers' and children's understanding. If the most powerful influence on children's number development is formal schooling, then the responsibility *must* lie with class teachers to ensure children learn number skills thoroughly and in appropriate contexts in school.

References

Aubrey, C. (1997) *The Processes of Mathematical Instruction in Children's First Year at School*. London: Falmer Press.

Balacheff, N. (1990) Towards a problématique for research on mathematics teaching. *Journal for Research in Mathematics Education*, 21(4): 258–72.

Carpenter, T.P. and Moser, J.M. (1982) The development of addition and subtraction problem-solving skills. In T.P. Carpenter, J.M. Moser and T.A. Romberg (eds), *Addition and Subtraction: A Cognitive Perspective*, pp. 9–24. Hillsdale, NJ: Lawrence Erlbaum Associates.

Carpenter, T.P., Fennema, E., Peterson, P.L., Chiang, C.P. and Loef, M. (1989) Using knowledge of children's mathematics thinking in classroom teaching: An experimental study. *American Educational Research Journal*, 26: 499–531.

Cobb, P. (1988) The tension between theories of learning and instruction in mathematics education. *Educational Psychologist*, 22(2): 87–103.

Fuson, K.C. (1988) *Children's Counting and Concepts of Number*. New York: Springer-Verlag.

Geary, D. (1994) *Children's Mathematical Development: Research and Practical Applications*. Cambridge: Cambridge University Press.

Kamii, C.K. (1989) *Young Children Continue to Re-invent Arithmetic Second Grade: Implications of Piaget's Theory*. New York: Teachers' College Press, Columbia University.

Lave, J. (1988) *Cognition in Practice: Mind, Mathematics and Culture in Everyday Life*. Cambridge: Cambridge University Prèss.

Murray, H. *et al.* (1993) Voluntary interaction groups for problem-centered learning. In *Proceedings of the Seventeenth International Conference for the Psychology of Mathematics Education*, Vol. II, pp. 73–80.

Nuñes, T., Schliemann, A.D. and Carraher, D.W. (1993) *Street Mathematics and School Mathematics*. Cambridge: Cambridge University Press.

THE PLACE OF COUNTING IN NUMBER DEVELOPMENT

The two chapters in Section 1 discussed the number understanding of children in nursery and reception classes, and counting was mentioned several times. This section of the book considers this particular aspect of number knowledge in greater detail, and places emphasis on the importance of counting for children throughout Key Stage 1 and even into Key Stage 2.

In Chapter 3, Effie Maclellan succinctly outlines some of the seminal research findings of American researchers Karen Fuson and Rochel Gelman. She describes in detail six different counting contexts in which young children experience number: sequence, counting, cardinal, measure, ordinal and non-numerical contexts. She also discusses Gelman and Gallistel's five counting principles: the one-one, stable-order, cardinal, abstraction and order-irrelevance principles.

She discusses some of the simple strategies that children use to find sums and differences of small collections. She argues that, although 'counting-up' for subtraction appears to be easier than 'counting-down', it is actually a more sophisticated strategy, depending, as it does, on the complementarity of the operations of addition and subtraction. The suggestion is made that teachers may need to teach the strategies of 'counting-on' and 'counting-up' explicitly so that these methods form part of their children's calculation repertoire.

Julia Anghileri (Chapter 4) explains how children's first experiences of multiplication arise when they make groups containing the same number of objects and realize that they can count the groups rather than the individual items. She uses examples of children's work to illustrate some of the potential language difficulties associated with the vocabulary of multiplication and division. She then charts the progression in multiplication and division skills that are evident in the early years classroom, and identifies links between the counting procedures that children use for solving addition and subtraction problems and those that they develop to solve multiplication and division problems. She suggests that teachers should help children to focus on the diversity of the language associated with equal grouping and sharing activities and on how such language may be related to counting patterns.

In Chapter 5, Ian Thompson provides a preliminary classification of derived fact strategies in addition, subtraction and multiplication based on those used by one hundred and three 6- to 8-year-olds. Transcriptions of children's idiosyncratic calculation methods are used to exemplify the classification. For addition the derived fact strategies comprise: counting-on, using doubles, bridging-up-through-ten, step counting and regrouping. The subtraction procedures include: counting-out, counting-down-from, counting-up-from and bridging-down-through-ten. Many of the examples illustrate the extent to which some children, even when they have learned number facts or more sophisticated calculation strategies, can combine these methods with counting techniques to ascertain unknown facts. This idiosyncratic merging of calculation procedures is lucidly illustrated with some creative solution strategies for multiplication.

Eddie Gray (Chapter 6) provides a link between this section and the next when he emphasizes the role that counting plays in enabling children to make the important shift in attention from objects in the real world to objects in the arithmetical world: a shift from practical manipulatives to numbers and their symbols. He distinguishes between the meaning of the terms 'process' and 'procedure', and introduces a new idea which he calls a 'precept' – a symbol which ambiguously represents both a process and a concept.

Gray stresses the importance of children compressing counting procedures to enable them eventually to make a choice between strategies, and argues that those who have succeeded in compressing counting procedures into known and derived facts have developed a powerful tool for success in arithmetic. Those who know facts and use them flexibly find arithmetic far easier than those who have to carry out lengthy counting procedures each time they make a calculation. The more successful children may still count but they use the strategy in more sophisticated ways.

He argues that children need to be helped to see number as a flexible entity, which can evoke either a mental object to be manipulated or a counting process to be carried out. Children are then likely to be able to build up unknown facts in a meaningful way. He stresses that teachers must help all children to achieve this flexible form of thinking, which is developed through the compression of number processes into concepts. The most successful children use the facts they know to derive the ones they do not know.

The importance of counting

Effie Maclellan

Introduction

Piaget dismissed counting as being of little value. He maintained that although young children could recite the number names, such activity did not help them in their construction of the concept of number. Instead, Piaget emphasized that to begin to understand that number is the abstract property of any class or set of objects, children had to recognize that perceptual alterations to sets of objects did not affect the numerosity of the set. The importance which was attached to these views resulted in educational recommendations which stressed the sorting and matching activities with which teachers of young children are so familiar. However, research over the last 20 years has investigated the role of counting in the development of number concepts, and the findings suggest that counting is both a more sophisticated and a more powerful phenomenon than was conceived of by Piaget.

The development of counting

The emergence of counting in children is complex and a bit messy. It can begin in children as young as 2–3 years of age (Gelman and Gallistel 1978) but takes a number of years to develop. A principal task for the young child is to learn that number words are used in different ways in our society and that these will have different meanings depending on the context in which they are used. Fuson and Hall (1983) argue that there are at least six different types of context in which young children are exposed to number words.

The counting contexts

In the *sequence* context, there is no intention to count any objects or 'things'. Instead, the intention is to produce a string of words in conventional order. Contexts which allow this to happen are nursery rhymes (one, two, buckle my shoe; one, two, three, four, Mary at the cottage door), counting to keep time as in, say, a game of hide-and-seek, or even counting to contain anger as in 'count to ten'. Learning the conventional sequence of counting words is not easy. As adults we have mastered the task and therefore may not appreciate how difficult its achievement is. For us there is now no cognitive effort in rehearsing even quite a long sequence, but try the first verse of Jack and Jill saying only every second word, or try saying the nursery rhyme backwards. This gives some idea of the task facing young children.

But more than that, children have to master an enormous range of number words. It seems that children learn the 1–10 range by rote, followed by 11, 12, 13. Fourteen is the first number word which has strong parallels with 4. Fifteen is different from 5 but 16, 17, 18, 19 follow the pattern of 6, 7, 8, 9. Then children have to master the decade names: 20, 30, 40, 50 and so on. Their association with 2, 3, 4, 5 is not discernible. Asking children to 'count' will demonstrate this. They frequently get stuck on the '9', but once they are provided with the next decade name they can continue without help until they need the following decade name. A more detailed account of this aspect of counting can be found in Thompson (Chapter 11, this volume).

While learning the conventional sequence of number names is not true counting, it is nevertheless a difficult task for children. With exposure to the sequence of number names and the experience of 'moderate amounts of sequence production activities' (Fuson and Hall 1983), many children can recite the number sequence to 100 by the time they are about 6 years of age. Other children will, of course, take longer to become proficient in this task.

In the *counting* context, number words are applied to objects in the real world. By counting (usually in concert with a caregiver) the number of peas on the plate or the number of sweets received or the number of stairs to reach the top flat, young children are exposed to a critical feature of the counting context, which is that there is coordination between a number word and the countable. This coordination often manifests itself (Gelman and Gallistel 1978) in pointing to, nodding at or physically moving the countables while 'saying' the number words. But there is room for error in this coordination. Children may count the same object more than once or may fail to count a particular object. Such errors may be errors of execution (to which even adults are prone) or they may be errors of understanding (which will be discussed later).

In the *cardinal* context the number word describes the numerosity of a defined set of objects. To begin with, children learn that particular number words are associated with particular referents in our language: that we have two hands and ten toes; that we wear two shoes; that there were three bears; that Cinderella had two ugly sisters; that there are seven days in the week. Children who use a number word correctly in the cardinal context may be able to count with understanding. However, this cannot be assumed. The children may just be associating the cardinal word with its referent and not with the numerosity of the countable collection. Children must evidence something more, which will be discussed later, to demonstrate cardinal understanding.

In the *measure* context, the number words describe the numerosity of the measuring units which have been used. The measurement of any object or entity will be on a continuous dimension (such as length, weight, time, distance, speed, volume), which has its own particular units of measurement. Children must therefore learn which are the appropriate units for each dimension but, more importantly, they must appreciate the level of precision which is required in using any particular measuring instrument. It is only when the measuring procedures have been followed to an agreed level of specificity that there is any point in counting the measuring units. There is little point in counting cups of flour if each cup is not completely filled. Equally, there is little point in using a measuring tape if the tape is not properly positioned. Without an understanding of this information, which is integral to the task of measuring, number words in the measure context can become confused with number words in the cardinal context. According to research reviewed by Fuson and Hall (1983), young children have great difficulty in making any coherent sense of the measure context.

In the *ordinal* context, as in the cardinal context, number words become associated with particular referents. In the ordinal context, the number word describes the relative position or the relative magnitude of a particular countable within a defined and ordered set of countables: so there was the first man on the moon or the second child in the family or the third fastest runner to complete the race. Fuson and Hall (1983) maintain that children experience number words in the ordinal context much less than they do in the cardinal context. It is thought that beyond first, second and third, children learn most ordinal words by deriving them from their cardinal equivalents, rather than as a distinct sequence.

In the *non-numerical* context, number words are used as identifying 'names' or codes. These contexts are ubiquitous in our society – for example, telephone numbers, room numbers, licence registration numbers – and have no real meaning.

According to Fuson and Hall (1983), any number word will, initially, be learned as several different words, each of which is tied to the context in which it is used. With repeated experiences, the different nuances of meaning are seen to be related to each other and so children learn that there are various meanings for any one number word. In so doing, the children construct the meaning of counting. They cannot explain this meaning in language which you or I would use but may be able to demonstrate this meaning through overt behaviour. But what is this meaning which children construct? Gelman and Gallistel (1978) suggest that the meaning is enumerated in five counting principles.

The counting principles

1 *The one-one principle.* Being able to count involves having an understanding of one-to-one correspondence in assigning a distinct counting word to each of the items in the array of countables. There must be a different counting word used for each item in the array. So in counting a three-item array,

the child who said 1, 2, 2 would not be demonstrating understanding of the one-one principle, whereas the child who said 1, 6, 2 would (by dint of giving each item a different name).

2 *The stable-order principle.* Being able to count also means knowing that the list of words used must be a consistent one. Since consistency is the essential property of the stable-order principle, some children may use their own idio-syncratic counting lists, but in using them reliably they are indeed demon-strating counting competence. The child who for one four-item array says 1, 2, 3, 4, but for a subsequent four-item array says 2, 1, 6, 7, does not have a grasp of the stable-order principle (although does have a grasp of the one-one principle). But the child who repeatedly counts a four-item array as 1, 3, 2, 6 and starts off more numerous arrays with the same sequence is evid-encing knowledge of the stable-order principle. Gelman and Gallistel (1978) found that children who used their own idiosyncratic lists 'were better able to apply the stable-order principle than were children who used conven-tional lists of number words'. We should not be surprised by this, since the conventional counting list is, in large part, quite arbitrary (as was discussed in the sequence context above) and it is much more likely that children would remember better lists of their own making than lists determined and imposed by others. Nevertheless, in the interests of arithmetical commun-ication, it is essential that children do learn the conventional sequence of number words.

3 *The cardinal principle.* Being able to assign a distinct number word to each countable and being able to do this consistently is not all that is involved in being able to count. A crucial component is the knowledge that numerosity is a property of all countable entities. In other words, counting is not merely a process in which one engages, but it can actually yield a product. Repeated practice in counting any given numerosity (always assuming that the one-one principle and the stable-order principle are being honoured) will ter-minate in the appropriate number word. When a child recognizes that this final number word has special significance, in that it is not only the last count word but that it also represents the numerosity of the set, the child has grasped the cardinal principle. Evidence for the cardinal principle having been grasped comes from how the child responds to the question, 'How many ___ are there?' There is some understanding of the cardinal prin-ciple when the child responds immediately and appropriately to the 'how many?' question, or when the child counts an array and repeats the last number word as in 1, 2, 3, 4, 4, or when the child counts an array and emphasizes the last word as in 1, 2, 3, **4**. On the other hand, when a child has no grasp of the cardinal principle, the child will respond to the 'how many?' question by recounting the array. In other words, such a child seems to view counting as a discrete activity which has no end-product. Per-haps the evidence (Saxe 1982, cited in Fuson and Hall 1983) which indicates mature understanding of the cardinal principle is the child's ability to indicate how many items of an array have been counted to date when the child is

stopped in the middle of a count. This shows that the child is aware that each successive number word has potential cardinal meaning.

Gelman and Gallistel (1978) view these three principles as the 'how-to-count' principles, since they specify the way to execute a count. The remaining two are 'what-to-count' principles which define, to the child, what can be counted.

4 *The abstraction principle.* This is the understanding that the how-to-count principles can be applied to any array or collection of entities, whether these are physical or non-physical, heterogeneous or homogeneous. While adults recognize that almost anything can be counted, there has been, historically, the view from developmental theorists that children first classify objects according to perceptual properties such as colour or shape and only later classify according to abstract properties such as number or function. This perception of how children learn to classify seems to have been understood as meaning that children could only count objects which were perceptually similar. Gelman and Gallistel (1978) argue that while children may well place restrictions on what is or can be counted, they do not limit themselves to counting collections of identical objects. Gelman and Gallistel (1978) maintain that there is no need to impute a complex and hierarchical classificatory scheme as being a prerequisite to counting because, in their view, the relatively crude distinction between 'things' and 'non-things' is sufficient to allow counting to be undertaken. All that this means is that children are perfectly willing to count collections of miscellaneous and heterogeneous objects and refer to them as 'things'.

5 *The order-irrelevance principle.* This final principle refers to the knowledge that the *order* in which items are counted is irrelevant. As long as all of the items in the array are counted and as long as each is counted only once, it matters not whether the counting is effected from left to right, from right to left or from somewhere in the middle. In having this knowledge, children have some awareness that number names are arbitrary and temporary designations rather than inherent properties of the countable items. These children will also know that the cardinal value of the array is not affected by the order in which the items are processed. Evidence that these children have grasped this principle comes from their being able to modify the order of enumeration, by treating a designated item as 'number one' and also taking account of all of the remaining items in the array. Confirmation of this comes from their justification that the number word assigned to any particular item depends upon the specific order of enumeration in any given count. This is not to say that the execution of the count will always be perfect, but then neither is it with adults.

According to Gelman and Gallistel (1978), when children have grasped the order-irrelevance principle, they know quite clearly what they are doing when counting. Furthermore, it is believed that many children have all of this knowledge by the time they start school. Careful observation of young children will show many of them counting spontaneously in what to adults would seem purposeless counting activities. Furthermore, they self-correct and perfect their counting with little direct input from adults. Historically, we have underestimated children's counting by failing to realize that counting develops, much like early language, through a process in which the child takes the initiative.

Implications for teaching and learning

Once children have the knowledge which underpins counting, not only can they make precise quantitative judgements (as distinct from exclusively perceptual judgements), they are also in the powerful position of being able to penetrate the tasks of addition and subtraction. For children who can neither retrieve the addition and subtraction 'facts' from memory nor derive new 'facts' from an existing repertoire, the only way in which they can find sums of, or differences between, numbers is to count. Clearly, many young children at the start of school will be in this position, but so too will many others who have been at school for a number of years. Indeed, some children will be totally reliant on counting to obtain answers to addition and subtraction operations during the entire period of primary schooling.

Having learned that counting is a meaningful strategy to solve addition and subtraction operations, there is the potential for the counting strategy to become elaborated into different procedures. Typically, when adding, children first use the procedure of counting all. A child will count out each set of objects (addends), combine the two sets into one new set and then count the objects in the new set. Extensive and repeated practice of counting objects eventually leads to the ability to use the counting words themselves as objects to count. That children learn that objects do not have to be perceptually present to be counted (but can instead be represented by the counting words) is highly significant, because this is evidence of the children having some (albeit primitive) knowledge of counting as mental activity.

A refinement of the counting-all procedure is the counting-on procedure where the child starts counting with the number name which represents the numerosity of one of the arrays to be added. Furthermore, the child may well be efficient and start with the larger array. In using the counting-on procedure, the child is both minimizing the amount of counting which has to be done and evidencing an understanding of cardinal meaning. The child could count each item in the array but to do so would yield no surprises to the child. Counting-on emerges from counting-all in some children who are as young as 4 years of age. It can be common in 6-year-olds but is not a procedure which is commonly taught by those teaching young children. Given that counting-on represents a qualitative advance in understanding, and given that the available evidence suggests that those children who have learning difficulties in mathematics are 'tied' to the most rudimentary of counting procedures, it would seem to be important to ensure that the procedure of counting-on is part of each child's repertoire. Interestingly, both Fuson (1982) and Carpenter and Moser (1982) have noted that children may use the counting-all procedure when they have already demonstrated proficiency in using the counting-on procedure. Carpenter and Moser (1982) imply that we unwittingly encourage this by the ready availability of physical entities for counting. Perhaps, then, we need to review the appropriateness of physical counting aids always being available?

An early counting procedure for subtraction is to count out the initial quantity (the minuend), remove the specified number of objects from the array (the subtrahend) and then recount what is left. Again, with increased understanding, this can give way to more sophisticated procedures. One such procedure is counting-down, where the child initiates a backward counting sequence, starting from the minuend and continuing until each member of the subtrahend has been accounted for. So in using this procedure for finding the difference between four and two, the child will verbalize '4 . . . 3, 2'; or in finding the difference between seven and three will verbalize '7 . . . 6, 5, 4'. The backward counting sequence contains as many number words as the given smaller quantity and the last name uttered in the sequence is the answer.

A more sophisticated procedure still is counting-up. Here the child initiates a forward counting sequence, starting from the subtrahend and ending with the minuend. So in finding the difference between four and two, the child will verbalize '2 . . . 3, 4', or in finding the difference between seven and three will verbalize '3 . . . 4, 5, 6, 7'. The number of counting words uttered in the sequence has to be kept track of by the child because it is this number which represents the difference between the initial numerosities.

While counting-down corresponds to the most basic way of thinking about subtraction – the notion of taking away – counting-up is a more sophisticated way of thinking about subtraction. Counting-up construes subtraction as complementary addition. This (albeit, initially implicit) knowledge of the complementarity of addition and subtraction is powerful arithmetical information. According to Resnick (1989), children can have control of both counting-down and counting-up by about 9 years of age. It seems that when children can choose which of the two procedures to use, they will elect to count up because they find this easier. However, counting-down is widely observed in children aged 3–13 years. Resnick (1983) maintains that the more sophisticated procedure is not explicitly taught to children at a sufficiently early stage of their primary education. What this means is that without explicit teaching of counting-up, children are essentially 'deprived' of this resource until such time as their understanding of the relationship between numbers allows them to see for themselves that addition and subtraction are inverse operations. The potentially lengthy time taken by children to discover for themselves (as against the shorter time which might be needed for systematic teaching) that counting-up is an appropriate procedure for subtraction operations, may well account for the fairly common finding that subtraction is more difficult than addition for young children. Indeed, such a position is supported by the findings of Fuson and Fuson (1992), who found that children were as fast and as accurate when subtracting as when adding provided that counting-up was used for subtraction and counting-on was used for addition.

Conclusion

There is now little doubt that children's understanding of number is rooted in counting. It is also clear that because counting develops from a very early age, many children will have fairly sophisticated understandings when they start school, as Aubrey (Chapter 2, this volume) demonstrates. This is not to suggest that children will be perfectly proficient in computation. Nor is there any suggestion that children can articulate their knowledge about number. Children will still need the teacher's help and they will still need structured activities. But the evidence does now suggest that there should be a sharp focus on counting. Since children find counting an intrinsically satisfying activity, there need to be many opportunities for counting to be practised in the different contexts. Furthermore, the amount of practice and experience of counting which young children need may be so extensive that perhaps parents can be appraised of the value of counting. The different counting procedures need also to be accorded their appropriate place. There is nothing to be lost, and indeed much to be gained, from explicit teaching of the counting procedures. The pedagogic issues turn on knowing which procedure a child is habitually using to make some judgement as to whether the particular procedure being adopted is enabling or hindering the child. Finally, if teachers are to support children in their counting endeavours, it may mean that pedagogic practices which are based on dated and incomplete accounts of number development should be reviewed.

References

Carpenter, T. and Moser, J. (1982) The development of addition and subtraction problem-solving skills. In T. Carpenter, J. Moser and T. Romberg (eds), *Addition and Subtraction: A Cognitive Perspective*, pp. 9–24. Hillsdale, NJ: Lawrence Erlbaum Associates.

Fuson, K. (1982) An analysis of the counting on procedure. In T. Carpenter J. Moser and T. Romberg (eds), *Addition and Subtraction: A Cognitive Perspective*, pp. 67–8. Hillsdale, NJ: Lawrence Erlbaum Associates.

Fuson, K. and Hall, J. (1983) The acquisition of early number word meanings. In H. Ginsburg (ed.), *The Development of Mathematical Thinking*, pp. 50–107. London: Academic Press.

Fuson, K. and Fuson, C. (1992) Instruction supporting children's counting on for addition and counting up for subtraction. *Journal for Research in Mathematics Education*, 23: 72–8.

Gelman, R. and Gallistel, C. (1978) *The Child's Understanding of Number*. Cambridge, MA: Harvard University Press.

Resnick, L. (1983) A developmental theory of number understanding. In H. Ginsburg (ed.), *The Development of Mathematical Thinking*, pp. 109–57. London: Academic Press.

Resnick, L. (1989) Developing mathematical knowledge. *American Psychologist*, 44(2): 162–9.

4

Uses of counting in multiplication and division

Julia Anghileri

Making groups and the importance of language

Children's first experiences of multiplication arise where they make groups with equal numbers of objects and recognize the possibility of counting the groups rather than counting individual items. Where there is a 'natural' link between the objects, like *pairs* of shoes or *sets* of wheels for model cars, this counting in groups is easiest; a line of shoes may be counted as individual items or as pairs, and the numerical connection is multiplication. Division is also practised by very young children as they share any collection into equal portions or divide a set of objects into equal subsets. Ideas of 'equal sets' and 'fair' portions are fundamental to an understanding of multiplication and division and these early activities can form a secure base from which understanding of the more formal operations with their specific language and symbols will be developed.

Everyday activities like laying places at a table involve grouping items and these groups can be counted. When a knife, a fork and a spoon are used for each setting, it would be somewhat artificial to count the individual pieces of cutlery, but the counting of groups may be associated with the number of people expected. Where there is no obvious link in the collection in each set, children must recognize the common property that enables groupings to be identified and must become aware of the importance of a one-to-one correspondence between the items in the sets. Repeating patterns will provide a visual image for equal groupings and opportunities to count items and sets of items. For a practical classroom activity, beads could be grouped in threes to make a coloured necklace. This would work equally well with repeated groups of different shaped beads or a 'Noah's Ark' activity with equal groups of different animals.

Much of the language used in talking about such activities is shared between multiplication and division (Anghileri 1995a), as the two arithmetic operations represent a different way of expressing the relationships that exist

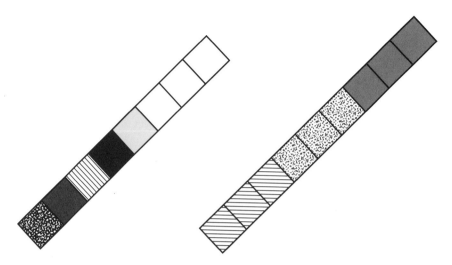

Figure 4.1 Incorrect responses to making a pattern stick with five colours
     using three of each colour
     – A stick with five colours and a further three cubes
     – A stick with three cubes in each of three colours

between three numbers. Whenever equal sets are put together and counted, reversing the procedure and reconstructing the original sets may be used to illustrate the way multiplication and division are inverse operations.

Early grouping and matching activities will encourage the use of important mathematical language, and although many people automatically think that this means words like 'multiply' and 'divide', there are more basic words that need to be understood before any formal language is introduced.

To illustrate some difficulties with language that may not be expected, consider the following observations and revealing responses from young children. Using pattern sticks made of linking cubes in different colours (Anghileri 1989), children were shown a stick using four colours with two cubes of each colour and asked, 'How many colours?' For many children the question 'How many . . .' led to a count of all the cubes and the response 'Eight'. When asked what the colours were, some children then realized the full implication of the question, but others were unable to count the groups and remained fixed on their understanding of eight cubes. When asked to 'make a pattern stick using five colours with three of each colour', common errors were to produce a stick with five different colours and a further three cubes added to the end, or a stick with three cubes in each of three colours (see Fig. 4.1). Not only was it difficult to identify the roles of the two numbers, five and three, but it was difficult for some children to recognize the importance of the word 'each' in the phrase 'three of each colour'. The word 'each' will be fundamentally important to understanding both multiplication and division.

One gets an idea of the scope and complexity of language when comparing such phrases as 'shared by three', 'shared with three', 'shared into three' and 'shared into threes'. Mathematical understanding will depend on detailed attention to the meanings of such phrases (and later phrases like 'divided by three', 'divided into three' and 'divided into threes') as it is clear that a collection like a bag of twelve apples can be divided differently 'by three', 'into three' and 'into threes' (see Fig. 4.2).

As well as developing understanding of the numerical relationships involved in multiplication and division, teachers will need to help children to focus on this language and the associated meanings. In practical situations, the ideas of multiplication and division as inverse operations may be explored: a collection that is made up by putting together four groups of three may be partitioned again into four groups, or into three groups or just two groups. Such grouped collections can be counted in various ways and links in the numbers explored so that children begin to build up their understanding of the number relationships. Where teachers recognize the wealth of relationships that can be found through such activities, they can guide children into appropriate use of language and begin to identify the arithmetic links that will be represented symbolically in later years.

Before 'multiplication' as a mathematical word is introduced, children may build up many ideas associated with 'equal sets' of objects, many 'lots of' items or actions, and experiences repeated 'many times'. For division, associated early language will involve 'sharing out' items to get 'equal portions', or 'dividing up' a collection with appropriate focus on words like 'each' and 'equal sets' and sometimes 'left-overs' and 'remainders'.

Patterns of numbers

As well as developing the language needed to understand multiplication and division, young children will begin to learn the number patterns that are especially important. For most children, counting sequences like 2, 4, 6, 8 . . . will become familiar at an early age and a lot of satisfaction may be achieved by mastering this and other more difficult patterns of multiples. Number rhymes like 'One, two, buckle my shoe. . . .' and 'One two, three, four, five . . . once I caught a fish alive' are enjoyed by children and encourage rhythmic pattern-making and counting. Both rhythmic counting in ones and *step* counting in multiples will provide useful strategies for solving multiplication and division problems. Rhythmic counting with emphasis on some numbers will provide a link between the two, and by building on children's understanding and recognizing significant stages in the development of counting, teachers can encourage children to learn these patterns and the relationships that provide a framework for later formalization. It is

12 apples divided into threes   12 apples divided into three

Figure 4.2 Illustration of the complexity of the language of division

not to say that multiplication has been mastered when the patterns of numbers become familiar, but that these may form the foundations of subsequent work enhancing children's overall number sense. It is not only for multiplication that these patterns are important; for example, the pattern of tens, '10, 20, 30, 40 . . .', is important for developing understanding of place value, and the pattern of fives, '5, 10, 15, 20 . . .', builds children's understanding of the role of five beyond the numbers they can easily count.

Counting procedures for multiplication

Step counting and rhythmic counting are used when children have a large collection of items to count and the rhythm can act as an aid to memory. When children have been closely observed finding the total number of objects arranged in equal groups, it is evident that there is a gradual progression from counting individual items to more rhythmic counting and ultimately recognition of the significance of a number pattern. Earliest uses of a counting strategy involve a count of every individual item in a unitary counting procedure (counting in ones). Often this is accompanied by some tactile reinforcement, like touching the objects being counted or using fingers to keep a tally. It is helpful at this stage to encourage the systematic arrangements of objects so that the idea of a repeating pattern and a rhythmic count become familiar. At this stage, some children will answer simple multiplication problems by using their fingers to model their mental image.

At the next stage, this unitary counting becomes rhythmic with developing emphasis on the group subtotals:

1, 2, **3** . . . 4, 5, **6** . . . 7, 8, **9** . . .

Again, some physical reinforcement like a nod of the head often accompanies this counting and children may start to use their fingers in growing independence from concrete objects.

It is interesting to observe the different ways that children use their fingers (Anghileri 1995b) and the balance between tactile and visual support that is provided as children develop mental imagery in their counting. In an investigation of children's solution strategies (Anghileri 1989), junior school pupils' responses were recorded when they were presented with practical tasks involving multiplication of single-digit numbers. One of the tasks involved a card with one-pence coins stuck on it in a regular 6×3 array. After some discussion about the number of coins in each row and in each column, the card was turned over so that the coins could no longer be seen. After checking that the children remembered the number of rows and the number of coins in each row, individual children were asked to figure out how many coins were on the card altogether. Many different ways of counting and using fingers were observed and difficulties sometimes arose over the differing roles of the two numbers. A typical example was Jenny (aged 8 years and 11 months), who used three different finger methods in her attempts:

Attempt 1. Having counted the middle three fingers of her left hand, 'One, two, three', Jenny raised one finger on her right hand as a tally. She focused again on her left hand to count, 'four, five, six', and raised a second finger on her right hand. Using her left hand she counted, 'seven, eight, nine'. When she raised a third finger on her right hand, her gaze passed from the right-hand three fingers to the left-hand three fingers and back again. At this point, she abandoned her first attempt, apparently confused over the differing roles of the fingers on her right and left hands.

Attempt 2. Jenny counted rhythmically three fingers at a time, starting on her left hand and then proceeding onto her right hand and back to her left hand. She counted, 'One, two, **three**'. She then used the remaining two fingers of her left hand and one finger of her right hand to count, 'four, five, **six**'. She continued this rhythmic counting in threes until she reached 'twenty-seven', when she was interrupted and asked to recall the structure of the array she had seen.

Attempt 3. She now started again with three fingers of her left hand, 'One, two, three'. She clasped these together saying, 'one lot'. Now she extended the remaining two fingers of her left hand and one from her right hand saying, 'one, two, three . . . two lots'. She proceeded in this manner working across both hands, counting in ones all the fingers she extended, '. . . one, two, three . . . six lots'. Now she went back to the beginning and successfully counted in ones all the fingers she had extended for grouping, 'One, two, three, four, five, six, . . . sixteen, seventeen, eighteen'. (She must have memorized all the fingers she had raised.) In this final attempt, Jenny had kept a mental tally of the sets of fingers she had raised and counted in ones all eighteen.

Roles of the fingers

This example illustrates how finger methods for multiplication are more complex than for addition and subtraction because the two numbers have differing roles: one represents the number of items in a set, whereas the other represents the number of such sets (and sometimes a ratio between two sets). As in Jenny's first attempt, the fingers on different hands may be used to designate two very different counts that are taking place concurrently.

When counting of repeated sets is to be used as a solution strategy for multiplication, there are *three* concurrent counts that must be undertaken. Two such counts relate to the individual items: a primary count matches a counting word with each item, while a matching, internalized count monitors the fact that every set has the same number of elements.

Verbal count	1, 2, 3 . . .	4, 5, 6 . . .	7, 8, 9 . . .	10, 11, 12
Internal count	1, 2, 3	1, 2, 3	1, 2, 3	1, 2, 3

Here the fingers can give tactile and visual support to the matching count, allowing more attention to be focused on the ongoing count with the task of 'counting-on' from a subtotal. A third count is necessary to 'tally' the number of sets that have been accounted for.

Verbal count	1, 2, 3, . . .	4, 5, 6, . . .	7, 8, 9, . . .	10, 11, 12
Internal count	1, 2, 3	1, 2, 3	1, 2, 3	1, 2, 3
Tally	1	2	3	4

This tallying must be done at the same time as monitoring the '1–2–3' count and it is this feature that causes problems for some children. In the case of Jenny, it is clear that in her second attempt she is maintaining two of the counts to produce groups of three numbers but is unable to implement the third 'tally' count. In her third attempt, Jenny found it more successful to keep repeating '1, 2, 3' as she kept a tally of the sets; she then went back to count the total number of fingers extended in her count. Other children's counting procedures often involve a greater degree of abstraction, as they are able to keep a silent tally of the sets or are able to count using a number pattern (e.g. 3, 6, 9, 12 . . .). The use of number patterns effectively reduces to two the number of concurrent counts to be maintained.

Children's methods may not be the same as those methods taught or those recommended in the schemes, but frequently involve 'invented' strategies that can be fascinating to watch. It is tempting to dismiss many of these strategies as inefficient and to attempt to replace them by the more conventional algorithms of arithmetic. It is true that more efficient strategies will need to be developed, but fingers often provide an important link between practical and mental methods, enabling abstraction to develop with understanding. For effective teaching of mathematics in the National Curriculum (DfE 1995), it is recommended that pupils are helped to develop flexibility and a range of methods for doing calculations. Teachers may encourage discussion among pupils of the different solution strategies they use and take the opportunity to study their procedures to gain information of their understanding and develop teaching strategies to help them refine these methods.

When fingers are used to tally the number of groups counted, children have established a method for solving multiplication problems that is evident throughout the primary school years and beyond, as finger methods give access to widely used strategies for solving multiplication problems. Historically, finger methods for multiplication were used before pencil-and-paper algorithms became commonplace and 'advanced' methods of finger calculations were used by educated monks and priests. Watching children attempting arithmetic problems will give teachers an opportunity to *see* procedures that exemplify children's thinking and illustrate their stage of understanding.

Stages of development

Multiplication and division problems may be solved by building up repeated sets and the questions, 'How many objects in four sets of three' and 'How many threes are there in twelve', may both be tackled by counting-up repeatedly groups of three using gradually more sophisticated strategies. The development of these strategies appears to run in parallel with children's developing strategies for addition and subtraction. Concrete objects will be used first to *model* each situation as the items are grouped and counted. While still counting in ones, many children start to count *rhythmically*, placing emphasis on the subtotal numbers (1, 2, **3** . . . 4, 5, **6** . . . 7, 8, **9** . . .); sometimes the spoken word is accompanied by a pause, a nod of the head or some other physical movement. The development from uniformly counting in ones to rhythmic counting in groups indicates that the child has some appreciation that it is

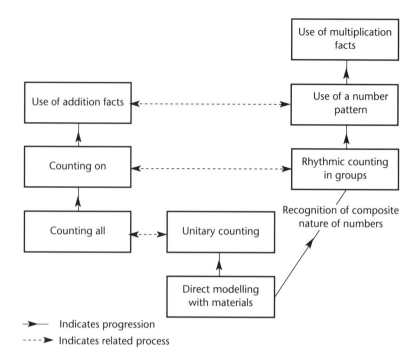

Figure 4.3 Relationships among addition and multiplication problem-
solving strategies

the sets that are to be tallied as the count proceeds from one set to the next.
This ability to *count on* from the total for each set has been noted as a stage
in the developing understanding of addition, where the child moves from
counting all of the objects to *counting-on* from the first subtotal. A more
detailed account of this strategy can be found in Maclellan (Chapter 3, this
volume). Next there is a stage of using number patterns which relates to the
use of number facts in addition. Finally, number facts are used directly or
related results are derived from facts that are known.

The links in a child's developing understanding of addition and of multiplication are illustrated in Fig. 4.3. Although the counting procedures for
addition and multiplication can be seen in many respects as developing in
parallel, multiplication is more complex, as it involves many groups and
each subsequent group to be counted must be constructed as a repeat of
the first group with a tally of the number of times it is used also kept. In
counting repeated sets, the child comes to recognize the need to terminate
one count and start the next corresponding count, continuing until the set
has been repeated a sufficient number of times. The transition from the first
stage (unitary counting) to the next stage (rhythmic counting) is marked by
the child's ability to recognize that the single word that ends the first count

represents the totality of the group – that is, transfer is made from the *counting* meaning of the word to the *cardinal* meaning (Gelman and Gallistel 1978; Fuson 1988) or recognition of the *composite* nature of numbers as well as the *component* nature (Steffe and Cobb 1988). This transfer has also been identified as the *cardinality* rule (Schaeffer *et al.* 1974).

Some children count rhythmically but only say out loud the subtotal numbers (the interim numbers being internalized, their presence being detected sometimes as a whisper, a silent mouthed acknowledgement or a time lapse to indicate that counting is taking place). In this manner, further emphasis is placed on the subtotal numbers, with the result that the number pattern produced becomes familiar in its own right.

The reciting of number patterns now becomes important for solving multiplication and division problems. Fingers may be used to tally the count but this method is much faster than counting in ones. Some children combine both a number pattern and counting in ones. When calculating how many counters there would be in six sets of three, Ruben (age 10 years 2 months) confidently began '3, 6, 9, 12 . . .', tallying by extending a finger each time to match the words. Now he continued '13, 14, **15**', extending a fifth finger, and '16, 17, **18**'. He did not look at his fingers or extend the sixth finger but knew immediately he was at the required total. Clearly, his use of fingers gave a *tactile* support to his internal calculations.

Each of the methods described above show successful children's strategies are often related to their use of fingers. These methods show the child's confidence in understanding the structure of multiplication or division and illustrate different stages of progress towards recognition of the importance of number patterns and multiplication facts. Very few children in the primary years appear to use multiplication facts directly (Anghileri 1989), although many have access to them when they are asked. The security of counting in ones, or in groups, and using fingers, somehow reinforces their understanding of the structure of a problem, giving them a model rather than an abstract fact.

Counting on the number line

Experiences with a number line will also help children to understand the nature of multiplication and division as counting in groups is related to a visual image of *equal jumps*. With encouragement to verbalize the numbers associated with different size jumps, this helps to reinforce the number patterns for multiplication and the way that counting groups may involve a tally of the number of jumps rather than the number of unit intervals involved. When the procedure is related to division, the number line is particularly helpful for counting 'backwards', since the patterns are not usually known in reverse. It can be helpful with division problems that do not give an exact answer, like 'How many threes are there in ten?', where remainders may be associated with the final interval that is shorter than the required jumps.

Counting the equal-sized intervals from a given number back to zero will involve a count in which the order of the number is increasing with progress to the left and a count which does not correspond to the numbers attached to the number line itself. This will be confusing for some children, but work with a number line may provide teachers with ideas for diagnostic assessment to establish understanding of the procedures for multiplication and division and the relationships between them.

Research in The Netherlands (Streefland 1991) has shown that the 'empty number line' with no intervals and no numbers marked enables children to be flexible in the size of jumps required and can be used to illustrate jumps of fifty or a hundred as easily as smaller jumps. Since the children may decide the starting and stopping points and need not work to scale, they are able to develop mental imagery that goes beyond the unit intervals normally found on number lines.

Division by sharing

In division, progression in counting will also be seen in sharing activities which form an alternative basis for division. Sharing and grouping are different procedures for dividing up a set. In the first instance, children must learn to either group objects, or to share equally and systematically, but they must also be helped to understand the way both procedures relate to division. It is not necessary to count in order to share equally and a common experience for young children is for them to undertake the practical sharing activity as an adult or more experienced child verbalizes an accompanying count. Again the emergence of rhythmic counting will enable children to begin to establish links between multiplication and division.

With large numbers of articles to be shared, a more efficient procedure that children will adopt is to share two or three at a time. The ability to guess or estimate the size of portions will help to identify a link between sharing and grouping, which will be necessary to solve such problems as one hundred shared between fifty. For such problems, sharing out one at a time between fifty portions will not be appropriate.

Implications for teaching

Counting involves skills that are successfully mastered by most children who can remember the consistent sequence of words and their association with numbers. Counting in multiples (e.g. 2, 4, 6, 8 . . . or 3, 6, 9, 12 . . .) also relies on memorizing consistent sequences of words that have a rhythm and pattern that can become very familiar. When these counts are associated with repeated groups of objects or equal intervals on the number line, they form a sound base upon which ideas of multiplication and division can be built.

Teachers can help children to focus on the diversity in language associated with equal groupings and sharing activities and how such language may be related to counting patterns. The particular words and procedures that enable children to solve practical problems will need to be refined to include more formal language, but the links that exist between multiplication and division must not be lost.

Children can show considerable initiative when attempting real problems that are presented to them within a familiar context. Opportunities for discussion will encourage comparisons between their different methods and may be used to focus on details of language that will be crucial for the precision needed in mathematics. It should be remembered that fingers are always available to support growing abstraction, which will facilitate progress with understanding. Confidence is crucial for successful problem-solving and the development from naive strategies to more formal and efficient procedures should not be at the expense of understanding or the gains may be very short term.

References

Anghileri, J. (1989) An investigation of young children's understanding of multiplication. *Journal for Research in Mathematics Education*, 20: 367–85.

Anghileri, J. (1995a) *Children's Mathematical Thinking in the Primary Years*. London: Cassell.

Anghileri, J. (1995b) Children's finger methods for multiplication. *Mathematics in School*, January, pp. 40–2.

Department for Education (1995) *Mathematics in the National Curriculum*. London: HMSO.

Fuson, K. (1988) *Children's Counting and Concepts of Numbers*. New York: Springer-Verlag.

Gelman, R. and Gallistel, C.P. (1978) *The Child's Understanding of Number*. Cambridge, MA: Harvard University Press.

Schaeffer, B., Eggleston, V. and Scott, J. (1974) Number development in young children. *Cognitive Psychology*, 6: 357–79.

Steffe, L. and Cobb, P. (1988) *Construction of Arithmetic Meanings and Strategies*. New York: Springer-Verlag.

Streefland, L. (1991) *Realistic Mathematics Education in Primary School*. Den Haag: CIP-Gegevens Koninklijke Bibliotheek.

The role of counting in derived fact strategies

Ian Thompson

Introduction

The idea that young children are capable of deriving unknown number facts from facts that they already know only really gained a hold in this country in the mid-1990s. This was despite the fact that American writers such as Carpenter and Moser (1984) and Steinberg (1985), as well as British writers like Thompson (1989, 1990) and Gray (1991), had written about this phenomenon some time earlier. In 1991, the year of the first Standard Assessment Tasks (SATs) for 7-year-olds, the guidance notes for teachers provided by the School Examinations and Assessment Council included the following advice: 'It is important that you assess each child's ability to add and subtract by using recall of number facts only, not by counting or computation'.

At that time, the appropriate National Curriculum attainment target required that children should 'Know and use addition and subtraction facts up to 10' (or 'to 20' at Level 3). The SAT guidance explained that 'know and use' meant that children should not be using computation in any obvious way to arrive at their answers, and that evidence of attainment could only be shown if the number facts were known by the child and produced spontaneously. One is inclined to ask what had become of the 'use' part of the attainment target! It seems somewhat perverse that a child who has found 4 + 5 by arguing that 'four and four is eight, so it must be nine' has been penalized – rather than being rewarded – for not only 'knowing' a number fact, but also 'using' it! The Ofsted (1993) report, *The Teaching and Learning of Number in Primary Schools*, mentions the importance of children using their own methods, but does not discuss these methods. Neither does it make specific reference to children deriving facts from other facts.

One of the first references to this strategy in official publications appeared in Askew and Wiliam (1995). This booklet comprises a review of recent research into effective mathematics teaching. In a section discussing 'knowing by heart' and 'figuring out', the authors state that: 'It seems then that pupils with access to both recalled and deduced number facts make more progress because each approach supports the other . . .'. In 1995, a further rewrite of the National Curriculum – often known as the Dearing version – appeared, and included several references to 'flexibility' and 'variety of methods' for children in all the key stages. The following quotation from this document clearly illustrates the shift in emphasis that had taken place: 'Pupils should be taught to . . . develop a range of mental methods for finding, from known facts, those that they cannot recall . . .'. Similar references to 'flexibility' are to be found in the Scottish Office Education Department's (1991) National Guidelines *Mathematics 5–14*.

Carpenter and Moser (1984) have identified the following levels of addition strategies used by young children when solving simple word problems: counting all, counting on from the first number, counting on from the larger number, using known number facts and using derived number facts. Many of these procedures are discussed in other chapters of this book. In this chapter, I shall attempt a preliminary classification of 'derived fact strategies' based on those used by fifty-nine children from Year 2 (6- to 7-year-olds) and forty-four from Year 3 involved in a small-scale research project investigating mental calculation strategies. The children were from three different schools in the Newcastle upon Tyne area.

Derived-fact strategies

The following classification of calculation methods for addition, subtraction and multiplication has been developed from an analysis of the transcripts of taped interviews. Several of the examples illustrate how some children, even when they have learned more sophisticated calculation strategies, occasionally combine these with counting techniques.

Addition

A wide range of addition strategies was generated by the children in this study, and examples were found of each of the types identified by Carpenter and Moser (1984). These methods are discussed under the following headings: counting-on, doubles, bridging-up-through-ten, step-counting and regrouping.

Counting-on

Many children used some form of 'counting-on' method, either as a basic strategy in its own right or as a technique to use as part of a more sophisticated strategy. A 'counting-on-from-first' strategy is clearly illustrated in Jacqueline's correct attempt at finding 5 + 6:

   5 . . . 6 . . . 7 . . . 8 . . . 9 . . . 10 . . . 11. It's eleven.

On the other hand, Steven's explanation of how he found his answer to the same problem illustrates how the drive for 'cognitive economy' – the desire to reduce the load on working memory – obliges him to adopt the 'counting-on-from-larger' strategy, while at the same time showing that he has some awareness of the commutative property of addition (5 + 6 = 6 + 5):

> Well, I took the big number first . . . I said six in my head and counted five more.

This use of commutativity becomes a more helpful labour-saving device as the difference between the two numbers to be added increases in size. One or two children extended 'counting-on-using-fingers' by involving imaginary appendages. Emma's response to 11 + 12 was:

> 23 . . . I had 12 and I added 10 on and a 1 . . . I didn't have enough fingers . . . I just said one more.

This 'finger-extension' strategy will be considered again in the section dealing with subtraction.

Doubles

This was the most common 'derived-fact' strategy used by the children, and is clearly illustrated in Hannah's answer to 5 + 6:

> I looked back in my memory . . . six and six is twelve, so it's one less.

Some children had favourite doubles which they used in a variety of situations, while others used a doubles fact and then used counting-on. Ben (finding 5 + 7) said:

> 10 . . . 11, 12. I counted in my head.

He actually counted aloud, but when pressed it transpired that he meant that he had doubled and then counted on two more. It is probably the case that other children use this calculating strategy, but the fact that they perform the count silently in their heads means that no-one else becomes aware of this.

Other responses involved a 'doubles-plus-or-minus-one' or a 'doubles-plus-or-minus-two' approach. Jane was seen to put up three fingers while working out 7 + 4 and, when asked how she arrived at her correct answer, replied:

> Four and four is eight . . . and then if you put a seven instead of the four it's three more . . . so it's three more than eight.

This extension of the basic 'doubles-plus-or-minus-one' to a 'doubles-plus-three' strategy was much more rare!

Bridging-up-through-ten

The mathematical idea underlying this strategy is 'complements in ten'. For example, 7 is the complement in ten of 3, and 1 is the complement of 9. This idea is covered in most mathematical schemes by the 'story of ten' type of activity, but very few of these schemes offer more than one or two such activities. The concept is not usually treated as the important building block for mental arithmetic that it would appear to be. Vicki worked out 8 + 5 by, in her own words,

... taking the two off it and putting it there.

Clearly, she had decided to make the eight into a ten by adding the two that she had removed from the five. The subsequent addition of the ten and the three was then more easy for her to do. Paul's explanation of his answer to the same problem was:

I made the eight into ten and went 11, 12, 13.

To use this strategy effectively, children need to be able to do the following: ascertain what is needed to build one of the numbers up to ten; partition the other number into two appropriate parts, and then add these two parts separately by counting-on or by making use of their knowledge of the effect of adding a single digit number onto ten. The 'complements-in-ten' strategy, with or without counting, was used much more frequently with subtraction than with addition, and is considered in more detail below.

Step-counting

Counting in multiples of two, three or indeed any number is what is meant by 'step-counting'. Children often learn this skill, and some teachers teach it, as a preparatory activity for the learning of 'tables facts'. Ben's answer to the calculation 4 + 5 was:

4 ... 6 ... 8 ... 9.

It was difficult to ascertain exactly why Ben had tackled the problem in this way, but it related to his visualizing the five in standard 'domino' formation, then adding the two pairs of dots by counting on in twos from four, and finally adding on the remaining dot. He later used a similar strategy when calculating 13 + 15:

33 ... I counted in fives after fifteen and added three on.

Ben had actually counted on one five too many using this method.

It is interesting to note that children appear to make errors very rarely when using their own personal heuristics. However, an analysis of the thinking involved in Ben's solution suggests a potential source of error. He first had to recognize that fifteen was an element in his five times table and that thirteen comprised two (or perhaps just 'some') fives and a three. Once he started counting on from fifteen in fives he also had to keep track of the number of fives he was counting. One possible reason for his error is that he was distracted by the fact that the number he had begun counting from (i.e. fifteen) contained three fives, and so this made him count on three rather than two fives. The fact that several children used this strategy suggests that 'step-counting' and the more difficult 'step-counting from different starting points' are useful activities for teachers to use in interactive whole-class or small-group mental arithmetic sessions.

Regrouping

This strategy is similar to the regrouping or decomposition method of subtraction. It involves the breaking down of one or more of the numbers into parts and then proceeding to operate with or on the various parts. The 'bridging-through-ten' strategy discussed above could be described as a 'regrouping' procedure. However, with larger numbers these parts, more often than not, comprise the tens and the units. In the research reported here, the tens were operated on *before* the units in 95 per cent of cases. A good illustrative example is Lucinda's lucid explanation of her method for finding the solution to 35 + 26:

> I added three and two up first . . . that's fifty . . . Five and six is eleven, so I took a ten off and made it to a sixty . . . and I made it to sixty one.

Lucinda not only uses regrouping as an overall strategy for the problem, but she also uses it in the middle of the calculation to deal with the extra ten she has obtained from adding the units.

Alan could not put into words how he had solved 27 + 28, but his actual answer reveals his thinking quite clearly:

> 40 . . . 47 . . . 48 . . . 49 . . . 50 . . . 51 . . . 52 . . . 53 . . . 54 . . . 55.

He has regrouped to deal with the two twenties first of all; has put the seven from the twenty-seven onto the forty to give him forty-seven; and has then counted on the remaining eight to give him the correct answer. Rachel (25 + 14) proceeded in a slightly different manner. As she worked out her answer she said:

> 25 . . . 35 . . . 36 . . . 37 . . . 38 . . . 39.

She has regrouped the fourteen as a ten and a four, has added the ten on to the whole of the other number – rather than just the tens part – and has then counted on the remaining four.

Subtraction

It is important that children come to appreciate the connection between addition and subtraction. Technically speaking, they are inverse operations where one operation 'undoes' the other: adding five and then subtracting five has no effect. The implications of this are that every known addition bond provides information on two subtraction bonds. For example, because 7 + 4 = 11, then 11 – 7 = 4 and 11 – 4 = 7. This is very useful information to have, and children need a range of classroom experiences to help them see this relationship between the two operations. Beth's explanation of her correct answer to 7 – 4 uses this connection:

> Well, four and three makes seven . . . so it's three.

Anna explained her correct answer to 14 – 8 by arguing that:

> Two sevens are fourteen . . . so you take away another one.

It is also the case that children who would not normally use counting when solving addition problems could well still be using such methods for subtraction.

Four main strategies for dealing with subtraction situations were identified over and above the use of known addition bonds. These methods comprised: 'counting-out' (separating from), 'counting-down-from', 'counting-up-from' and 'bridging-down-through-ten'. The first two strategies occurred with greater frequency than the latter two.

Counting-out

This method involves the modelling – usually on the fingers – of the number to be operated upon (the minuend). The required number of fingers is set up and then the number to be taken away (the subtrahend) is removed either by counting the fingers down, or by using prior knowledge of finger totals. The remainder is then dealt with in a similar way. This strategy can involve some children in three separate forward counts, although many youngsters soon learn to set up or remove a given number of fingers quite quickly and then read off from their fingers how many remain. Instead of modelling in this manner, some children use a mental representation of the situation. Patrick, working out $7 - 3$, said:

Four . . . I just knock down skittles in my head.

Further into the interview, having just given the correct answer to $13 - 6$, he explained: 'I just had a game of skittles'.

This strategy can be very successful when dealing with numbers of ten or less, but because of a finger shortage problem, it is less useful with larger numbers. Many children perceive the need for a more sophisticated technique when dealing with numbers greater than ten. Others, however, show surprising ingenuity in modifying a strategy that has brought them success. Anna had been correctly using 'counting-out' to answer some simple subtractions, and was asked to calculate $11 - 6$ with a view to helping her to realize the inadequacies of this technique with these particular numbers. Fingers were set up and the correct answer was given. When asked how she had worked out the answer even though she only had ten fingers, she replied: 'I counted the newspaper'. Anna had used my newspaper, which was lying on the table, as the eleventh object in her collection. She proceeded to 'remove' that object first before returning to the familiar territory of her ten fingers to deftly take away the remaining five objects. She later calculated $15 - 9$ by imagining five extra objects.

Joanne, however, was the expert in this particular technique. The following explanations for three different subtractions reveal her creative talents and her apparent obsession with her bodily parts:

I used my two legs [$12 - 4$].

I used both strips of my track suit as well as my legs. You could use your arms and your legs instead [$14 - 6$].

I took that one away [points to one arm] ... then that [points to other arm] ... and then my head [13 − 7].

Counting-down-from

It seems to be the case that when children discover or invent a more powerful or less time-consuming method for solving a particular problem, they tend to use it in all situations where they feel confident with the numbers involved. However, they do sometimes 'regress' to less sophisticated methods on occasions where the numbers are unfamiliar or larger than those they are used to. This is to be expected, since most adults tend to operate in a similar manner. It is also true that they sometimes explain their methods to 'confused' researchers by referring to a 'simpler' strategy that they may well have abandoned at an earlier stage in favour of a less time-consuming method. 'Counting-down-from' can be used to deal with all those subtractions easily solved by using 'counting-out', but it also has the advantage of being more effective for the solution of problems involving numbers greater than ten. Richard found 7 − 3 by saying:

7 ... 6 ... 5 ... 4.

while putting up three fingers, and Rebecca correctly worked 23 − 9 by counting backwards starting from 22 and tallying the count on nine of her fingers.

This strategy was the most common subtraction procedure used by the children in this sample. However, an analysis shows that it is quite a sophisticated strategy. Children need to be able to execute successfully the following sub-skills: count backwards from a specified number; count backwards a specific number of steps; and employ some suitable 'keeping track' device. In addition, they must also have already perceived a need to keep track of the numbers being counted. Fuson (1988) has provided a detailed breakdown of the various keeping-track methods used by children when counting-on and counting-back.

Baroody (1984) argues that, because this procedure involves a forward count during the keeping-track phase, 'counting-down-from' involves two simultaneous processes which in effect go in opposite directions. This fact could account for the occasional errors that were made by children using this technique. Graham gave the answer 'five' when finding 7 − 3. His counting back strategy had let him down because he had counted '7 ... 6 ... 5' instead of '6 ... 5 ... 4', an error made by one or two other children in the sample. The backward and forward count and the keeping-track method had all been correctly executed. Graham had simply started his count at the wrong place. Some Year 3 children used this strategy in connection with their place-value knowledge to tackle more difficult two-digit subtractions. Daniel found 33 − 18 in the following way:

It was 33 and I took away the ten ... that was 23 ... then I took away the eight.

When asked how he had taken away the eight, Daniel replied that he had counted back in his head. There were other children who used this extension of the standard strategy.

Counting-up-from

Carpenter and Moser (1984) suggest that children prefer to use the 'counting-up-from' rather than the 'counting-down-from' strategy – what used to be called 'shopkeeper arithmetic' when tills did not tell you how much change to give. This does appear to be borne out by their data, since only 18 per cent of their sample did not use this strategy at all. Baroody (1984), on the other hand, argues that children use the 'counting-down-from' strategy more frequently because it provides a more accurate model of their informal concept of subtraction as 'take away'. The results of my study confirm Baroody's (1984) position, since only *three* of the 103 children interviewed used this procedure. One possible explanation for the use of this strategy by so few children is that they were not given a context within which to do the calculation, but were – in the case of subtraction – asked questions like 'What is eleven take away two?' while simultaneously being shown a card with 11 – 2 written on it. The verbal format used presents the situation as a 'take away', and perhaps thereby militates against the children using a 'counting-up-from' strategy.

A consideration of Gillian's answer to 7 – 3 should clarify the way in which this procedure operates:

3 . . . 4 . . . 5 . . . 6 . . . 7 . . . It's four.

The final part of her answer came from her reading off the number of fingers she had raised while tallying her forward count. Here we have a 'count-and-tally-and-then-count-the-tally' procedure. What is being counted in this case is the number of counting words from three to seven. This strategy demands that the finger that is normally mapped onto the counting word 'one' is, instead, mapped onto the word 'four'. This is quite a subtle adaptation of the basic counting procedure.

Bridging-down-through-ten

This strategy was used on many occasions and by a number of children. It employs aspects of two sub-strategies discussed in the section on addition: 'complements-in-ten' and 'regrouping'. Tim, working out 15 – 9, said:

I took away five from fifteen and then I took away four . . . that's six.

Vicki's account of how she calculated 23 – 9 provides a lucid explanation of the thinking involved in the execution of this procedure:

Three and six make nine . . . and I took three away to make twenty . . . and I had the six to make four . . . so it's fourteen.

Vicki mentions 'four' because it is the complement-in-ten of six.

None of the children in the sample had been taught this strategy by their teachers, and yet an analysis of the technique suggests that it is very subtle and quite complex. The units digit of the larger number tells you how many to take away first to reduce this number to ten or to a multiple of ten. You then have to break the smaller number into two parts, one of which is equal to the units digit of the larger number. The other part tells you how much you still have to take away from the ten (or multiple of ten). The answer is the complement-in-ten of this number or a multiple of ten added to this complement. Imagine trying to teach this technique formally!

One child combined this strategy with a counting procedure to obtain his answer. Daniel (24 − 7) explained his answer thus:

I took away four to twenty . . . then I took away three and I got seventeen.

When asked how he took away the three he said:

I went 20 . . . 19 . . . 18 . . . 17.

Had more children been asked how they tackled this final stage of the calculation it could well be that other similar examples would have come to light.

Multiplication

Many of the children in this study had experienced little work on multiplication. However, there were some whose grasp of number seemed sufficiently developed to warrant asking them a few basic multiplication questions. Consequently, the range of strategies was more restricted, although counting was very much in evidence. For example, to find, say, three sets of four, several children counted out all three sets on their fingers. Melissa's answer to this question was:

8 . . . 9 . . . 10 . . . 11 . . . 12 [doubling with counting on].

Rebecca took this strategy one stage further when she worked out 6 × 6 by first doubling six. She then doubled twelve, and finally counted in ones from 24 to 36. Some children found 4 × 5 by step-counting in fives. Charlotte's response to 4 × 6 used step-counting with counting-on:

6 . . . 12 . . . 18 . . . 19 . . . 20 . . . 21 . . . 22 . . . 23 . . . 24.

Both of these strategies were used quite often. Kevin gave an interesting answer to 6 × 6 when he said:

Something like 36 . . . six and six makes twelve . . . 24 . . . 36.

Other children used a known fact combined with some form of counting. For example, Camilla used a sophisticated procedure, but made an unfortunate mistake in the process. Her solution to 6 × 9, a hard calculation reserved for the more able Year 3 children, went as follows:

Fifty-one . . . six tens are sixty and then I counted down nine.

Her error came from counting down 'nine' rather than 'six', but her method of calculation was quite ingenious for someone only 7 years 8 months old! One of the most creative examples comes from Andrew, an obviously able 7-year-old. Asked to work out four lots of eight he explained his correct answer in the following way:

Three sevens are 21 . . . add on all the next ones to get eight . . . you have three more units, so you get 24. Add on eight and you get . . . 24, 25, 26, 27, 28, 29, 30, 31, 32.

These examples suggest that while they are gradually building up a repertoire of learned multiplication facts, children still rely heavily on a combination of doubles, step-counting, known facts and counting techniques to help them derive facts that they do not know. Anghileri (Chapter 4, this volume) provides a more detailed account of the role of counting in the early stages of learning multiplication.

Implications for teaching

Gray (Chapter 6, this volume) warns us of what he calls the 'proceptual divide', where those children who come to see numbers as mental objects that can be manipulated begin to diverge from those who remain wedded to procedural aspects – using counting as their only strategy and thereby making life more difficult for themselves. There is a possibility that Gray's analysis may be interpreted in some quarters as a call for a ban on counting and a demand for the drilling of 'tables' and 'number facts'. The research reported in this chapter, however, suggests that we do not have a simple dichotomy: counting versus fact learning. Inevitably, the issue is more complex: even those who are able to mentally manipulate numbers still occasionally have recourse to counting strategies, albeit of a more sophisticated nature than those involved in 'counting-on' or 'counting-back'. Teachers have to learn to distinguish between those children whose relatively unsophisticated counting procedures are impeding their progress and those who are using counting as part of a network of strategies to help them to derive new facts from known facts.

Askew and Wiliam (1995) argue that:

For some lower-attaining pupils it may be that over-dependence on counting methods . . . removes the need to commit number facts to memory, which in turn limits their development of deductive approaches.

Teachers need to listen to children's explanations of their personal calculation methods so that they can identify those children who persist in using counting as their sole strategy in all situations. They must ensure that these children, whether low-attainers or not, are provided with a wide variety of mathematical activities and teaching approaches that will afford them the opportunity to make their own connections; to commit some simple number facts to memory; and to develop the confidence necessary to use these facts to help them figure out number bonds that they have not yet learned by heart. Activities suitable for this purpose can be found in Wigley (Chapter 10, this volume), Thompson (Chapter 11, this volume) and Sugarman (Chapter 13, this volume).

References

Askew, M. and Wiliam, D. (1995) *Recent Research in Mathematics Education 5–16*. London: HMSO.

Baroody, A.J. (1984) Children's difficulties in subtraction: Some causes and questions. *Journal for Research in Mathematics Education*, 15(3): 203–213.

Carpenter, T.P. and Moser, J.M. (1984) The acquisition of addition and subtraction concepts in grades one through three. *Journal for Research in Mathematics Education*, 15(3): 179–202.

Fuson, K.C. (1988) *Children's Counting and Concepts of Number*. New York: Springer-Verlag.

Gray, E.M. (1991) An analysis of diverging approaches to simple arithmetic preference and its consequences. *Educational Studies in Mathematics*, 22(6): 551–74.

Ofsted (1993) *The Teaching and Learning of Number in Primary Schools*. London: HMSO.

Scottish Office Education Department (1991) *Mathematics 5–14*. Edinburgh: SOED.

Steinberg, R.M. (1985) Instruction on derived facts strategies in addition and subtraction. *Journal for Research in Mathematics Education*, 16(5): 337–55.

Thompson, I. (1989) Mind games. *Child Education*, 66(12): 28–9.

Thompson, I. (1990) Double up and double back. *Child Education*, 67(8): 36–7.

Compressing the counting process: developing a flexible interpretation of symbols

Eddie Gray

Arithmetical beginnings

In most infant classrooms during a mathematics lesson, we can see some form of counting. Children count counters, pencils, shapes, marbles, acorns, toys – anything. If it is countable it is counted. Counting is one of the actions young children participate in using everyday objects from the real world. Objects from this world can be seen. On the one hand, they are manipulated, named and described, providing the initial phases in the development of geometry; on the other, they can be quantified, giving the initial phases in the development of arithmetic.

Geometric growth stems from handling real-world objects. They are seen and manipulated, conceived of visually and holistically as they appear to the senses, and named. It takes time for the regularities of these shapes to be described in a more subtle verbal form, for their properties to be identified and relationships based on those properties to be established. Arithmetic also has a physical counterpart originating in the real world, so it has visual elements but it is possible for these elements to change. Actions on objects of the real world form objects that are part of the arithmetical world. However, whereas perception and manipulation lead to the gradual accommodation of geometric concepts, the formation of numerical concepts is far more subtle. It involves a shift in attention from the objects of the real world to the objects of the arithmetical world – numbers and their symbols.

The part that counting has to play in the shift of attention is the focus of this chapter. We will see how actions upon objects of the real world may be steadily compressed to form objects of the arithmetical world. Children who use the underlying strength of these new objects have a source of flexibility and power which provides them with a stepping stone towards further mathematical growth. Those who do not become trapped within the complexity of the actions and left bewildered as arithmetic and mathematics generally becomes ever more complex.

Counting plays a sophisticated and central role in the development of number concepts. But how is this done? If it is so fundamental, why is it that well into Key Stage 2 we may see some children still relying extensively on it to add and subtract – even to establish multiplication facts? Perhaps it seems natural that if so much energy and time is expended upon the development of sound counting skills within Key Stage 1, some children within Key Stage 2 appear to be reluctant to use alternative approaches. The more we work at remembering how to do something, the more we are likely to use the remembered approach; it is perhaps the case that the more we remember how to *do*, paradoxically, the less we may *know*.

'It will help you if you count'

It will prove fruitful to distinguish between the terms 'process' and 'procedure', which will be used extensively in this chapter. The word 'process' is used in a general sense, as in the 'process of counting', the 'process of addition', or the 'process of subtraction'. It need not be something that is currently being carried out in thought or by action; for example, we may speak of the process of addition without actually performing it. Nor is there any implication that the process must be carried out in a unique manner. For instance, the process of addition may be carried out by counting or by some other method. The term 'procedure' is used to describe a specific algorithm for implementing a process. Flexibility in carrying out a process will play a fundamental role in our story. Within simple arithmetic, counting may stimulate the growth of such flexibility but it may also inhibit it. How may such a contraction arise? What is it about counting that may cause such a paradox?

Try to visualize James. He is a small 5-year-old sitting among a group of similarly aged children carrying out counting activities. His voice carries above the others within the group '. . . five, six, *seven*'. There is silence as he then quietly writes. A closer examination of what he is doing reveals that he was adding 3 + 4 using his fingers to count-on from four. Now think of Joseph who is 8. He is also trying to add 4 + 3. He is sitting motionless but his lips are moving and, looking closely, we can see his eyes moving slowly from left to right. The lip movements stop and then start again. His eyes repeat their movement. This happens several times, and each time a little more tension is evident in the deep frown on Joseph's face. Eventually Joseph's teacher interrupts his concentration: 'Use counters or your fingers Joseph. It will be easier'. There is some relief on Joseph's face as he goes for the second option without making it too obvious – he uses his fingers under his desk. Why? He explained later that he '. . . wants to do things like the clever children. They do it in their heads'. Counting on his fingers under the desk helps him continue his subterfuge: it still looks as if he is doing things like the 'clever children'. The teacher shares his secret. It is almost as if they have entered into a conspiracy: the current difficulty has been sorted out because he has been told how to *do* the sum using an easier approach. On the next combination, however, we begin to see the lips move and the eyes roll. Again his teacher very quietly intervenes and suggests that he should use his fingers: '. . . it will help you understand what you are doing'.

Two children, both counting, but there is a tremendous difference in the quality of this counting over such a spectrum of age. The 5-year-old is experiencing counting as part of a programme of conceptual development which may eventually give him choices. Joseph and children like him are counting because they are unable to do anything else – they have no choice. Faced with a problem such as 4 + 3 they translate it into a counting action. They have had plenty of experience doing this: an addition or subtraction sign means count, albeit a different sort of counting. It can take so long to do the counting and get an answer that such children may not remember the numbers they started with. Once again they have practised a counting procedure. Simple arithmetic is about counting. Joseph didn't realize that when the other children were doing things in their heads, they were using methods that are far easier than his. Even when he has difficulty, he is advised to try an approach that is harder than theirs. That this is so was aptly explained by Amanda, who is 9:

> I find it easier *not* to do it [simple addition] with my fingers because sometimes I get into a big muddle with them [and] I find it much harder to add up because I am not concentrating on the sum. I am concentrating on getting my fingers right . . . which takes a while. It can take longer to work out the sum than it does to work out the sum in my head.

What insight from a child who herself is having difficulty with arithmetic. She focuses on the two features emerging from elementary arithmetic that could create a dichotomy: being able to *do* and *think* at the same time. Doing the first may get in the way of the second, but within the classroom environment there can be clear difficulties in making the choice:

> If we don't [use our fingers] the teacher is going to think, 'why aren't they using their fingers . . . they are just sitting there thinking' . . . we are meant to be using our fingers because it is easier . . . which it is not.
>
> (Amanda, age 9)

The dual face of numbers

Through their experience of a counting procedure, young children learn to associate a counting action with a sequence of number words. The last number word tells them how many things have been counted and, with familiarity, the child can use this number word to stand for countable items (see Maclellan, Chapter 3, this volume). So, when counting five objects, the child points to each object in turn and repeats the sequence of number words 'one, two, three, four, five'. The final five tells them that 'five' have been counted. Later when they hear the word 'five' or see the symbol '5', they may associate these things with five countable items.

One of the interesting things about numbers and, no doubt one that we all know but do not make explicit to the children we teach, is that we treat them as if they were real 'things' – 'five is half of ten', 'three and four make seven'. Though there is no need to associate these things with other, real-life, objects to make sense of them, we can do so if we wish.

Early counting experiences associate numbers with things. By doing so it is possible that for the learner the notion of *seven* lines may have qualitatively little difference to the notion of *straight* lines. Of course there is one difference, the first is the result of an action and is arithmetical, the second the result of perception and is geometrical. However, the word 'seven' and the word 'straight' may be associated with the objects to which they refer, they may be properties of the set of lines. To continue associating numbers with other objects is very limiting. To say 'my sister is *seven*' may have a similar quality to saying 'my sister is *tall*'. The seven is concretized by being associated with real items: the numbers are used as adjectives and associated with other nouns. Real power in arithmetic derives from not only being able to see this but also to see the numbers as nouns (i.e. as 'things'). When we do this we can establish relationships between the 'things', something even young children after their initial experience with counting can do. They will tell us that the things can be seen differently. Nicky (age 5) looked at the two expressions 2 + 1 and 1 + 2 and said, 'See those two, they are both the same, they're both three'. Paul, his friend, thought he could give all of the numbers that make five. He started by saying, 'Two things together make a number' and he quickly reeled of examples that make five: '. . . two and three, four and one, five and nothing'. He had some trouble with one and four but decided he could do it if he counted.

Within these two examples we see two different but complementary aspects of numerical symbols, whether spoken or written. They refer to countable items and they compress ideas that allow us to see other relationships. Those children that recognize symbolic ambiguity, which either triggers the re-creation of the number through a counting process or its use as a thing, have a very powerful tool at their fingertips. Those that don't, like Joseph, are more unfortunate – they only have half of the key available to them. Unfortunately, this is the most difficult half.

Compressing counting procedures

Children's growing sophistication in handling counting procedures may be seen as an example of a steady compression which can eventually permit choice between these and the use of number concepts. We can see this by considering the relationship between the addition process and the concept of sum in, for example, the addition of 4 + 3. The most elementary method used to carry out the addition process is to count four objects (1, 2, 3, 4), then to count three objects (1, 2, 3), then to put all the objects together and count the total (1, 2, 3, 4, 5, 6, **7**). This succession of three separate counting procedures is called 'count-all'.

The next stage occurs when it is realized that it is not necessary to count a set of four followed by a set of three. One of the numbers, 4 for example, may be seen as a number object and the child can simply *count-on* a further three numbers in the number sequence. The sum of 4 + 3 becomes **4**, 5, 6, 7. We may see 'count-on' as another procedure used to carry out the process of addition. It may be spontaneously constructed and 'invented' by children (Baroody and Ginsburg 1986), 'personalized' (Gray 1991), or 'taught' (Fuson and Fuson 1992).

An important aspect of the two counting procedures used to carry out the addition process is the procedural compression signifying a change from lengthy procedures associated with count-all, to the more contracted ones of count-on. However, the move from one to the other is not as simple as it seems. Count-on is a sophisticated double counting process. To calculate 4 + 3 requires not only counting on beyond 4 in the number sequence but also keeping a check that precisely three numbers are being counted. In the infant class, we may see some children using counters and others using fingers. Sometimes the only evidence that a child is counting comes from the close observation which shows a nodding head, moving eyes or moving lips. Joseph tried this but he couldn't easily keep two numbers in focus at once.

Of course we shouldn't pretend that count-all and count-on are the only classifications which describe the steady compression of counting procedures. Steffe *et al.* (1983) provide us with a clearer picture of the things children create when they count; they indicate a growing sophistication in the objects used. Children may even change the numbers around, start with the largest 'because it is nearer the answer' and count-on the smallest. Baroody and Ginsburg (1986) see this distinction not only as an important step on the way to learning more formal arithmetic but, they suggest, it also provides an indication of the child's efforts to reduce the number of steps and the time used to carry out the process. Clearly then, it is possible to provide even finer gradations than those that form the focus of this chapter. Recognizing them may provide insight into the way in which children's thinking is developing. Fixation on any one may provide a longer-term prognosis of the child's achievement in arithmetic and in mathematics as a whole.

It is not our purpose to dwell on the finer details but to provide a coarser analysis which may be useful within the classroom and provide a sense of where such procedures may lead to. It is the notion of 'compression' which helps us do this. Whichever form of classification we use – the coarse one or the finer gradations which give a more detailed picture – we see that with experience children compress lengthier procedures into shorter procedures. The procedure may not only be quicker but it is suggested that its operation also uses up less memory space and makes it more possible to link directly the inputs to the outputs – to *know* the solution.

Linked directly to 7, the sum of 4 + 3 becomes a 'known fact'. In any isolated incident it is not easy to distinguish whether or not such facts are meaningful or rote learned. The difference may only become apparent when such facts are decomposed and recomposed to give 'derived facts' (see Thompson, Chapter 5, this volume). For instance, we may use the fact that 4 + 3

= 7 to 'derive the fact' that 14 + 3 is 17. It would even be possible to use another known fact such as 4 + 4 to derive the sum of 4 + 3.

By considering the compression of counting procedures we can begin to see more clearly what the experiences we give children may be leading to and, more importantly, what this experience is telling them. Count-all and count-on evoke different processes of counting, while known facts can evoke the concept of sum. Consequently, when young children are presented with elementary number combinations such as 4 + 3, they can interpret the notation in two qualitatively different ways: as a *process* to do, which can be progressively compressed to be manipulated as a mental *object.*

The child who has compressed counting procedures into known and derived facts possesses a powerful tool with which to achieve success in arithmetic. If they encounter problems with larger numbers they are able to use the knowledge they already have. As combinations become more difficult, those who *know* facts and *use* them flexibly find arithmetic far easier than those who have to carry out counting procedures. For such children, subtraction may become just another way of looking at addition; it is relatively easy for the flexible child who can use a related addition fact.

Such flexibility can be seen in stark contrast to the difficulties experienced by children who use counting procedures. These procedures may be successful for simple combinations but they may become extremely difficult for larger numbers. Concrete materials can be used to support (or rather, avoid) the double counting that is so frequently a feature of children's difficulties. This can give the semblance of progress when little progress has actually been achieved and the subtleties of the double counting of the count-on algorithm have not been sufficiently well appreciated to be carried out without physical supports. Joseph's failure without concrete aids and his eventual success with them, albeit with small numbers, aptly illustrate this point.

The child who relies on count-on for addition is much more likely to use its inverse, count-back, for subtraction. This can be horrendously difficult even with some physical support. Consider Jenny who attempted to count-back 13 from 19 keeping a check on the double count by using her fingers:

19, 18, 17, 16, 15, 13 . . . 14, 15 . . . 14, 13, 12 . . .

It is surprising that she arrived at the correct solution. Though she almost immediately recognized her miscount at 15, this caused her some added difficulty: was she counting-up or counting-back? To overcome such difficulty, we often use a number line to help children count-back but this may have a fatal flaw. Counting-back on a number line may be no more than an example of single-counting, hardly more sophisticated than count-all, and it may not generalize into a flexible form of subtraction.

The numerical procept

The evidence suggests that there are two main interpretations of arithmetical expressions such as 4 + 3. One makes use of numerical concepts and relationships, while the other triggers the use of counting procedures. This leads us to an important feature of arithmetical symbolism. Not only does it provide a sense of what to *do* but also what to *know*.

Now we begin to see what is so special about arithmetical symbolism. It is really so very simple. Numerical symbols don't represent either a process or an object; they represent both at the same time. Consider, as an example, the symbol '5'. It can be written and it can be seen. It can be spoken and it can be heard. The symbol '5' represents the fusion of a number name with a counting process. We can recreate the counting process whenever we see the symbol or hear its name. But we can also use the concept of 'five' without any reference to countable items. Many different processes give rise to the object five. Not only the process of counting 'one . . . two . . . three . . . four . . . five . . .', but also the process of adding four and one, of adding three and two, two and three, of taking three away from eight, or two away from seven, of halving ten, and so on. All of these processes give rise to the same object. The symbol '5' represents a considerable amount of information, not least the counting *pro*cess by which it is named and con*cept* or idea by which it is used. Gray and Tall (1994) believed such a fundamental ambiguity deserved its own terminology. This is embraced within the notion of *procept*: a symbol which ambiguously represents both *pro*cess and con*cept*. There are many numerical symbols that evoke either process or concept:

- 3 + 4 is either the process of *addition* of 4 and 3 or the concept of sum 7;
- 3/4 can mean (among other interpretations) the process of *division* of 3 by 4 or the concept of fraction $^3/_4$;
- 3 × 4 represents the process of *repeated addition* and the concept of product 12.

Not all mathematical symbols are procepts but they do occur widely, particularly in arithmetic, algebra and aspects of higher mathematics. We may consider number as a procept: as a process and as a concept, both of which are represented by the same symbol. Children who use count-all recreate the process embedded within each symbol. Children who use count-on may use either the process or the concept: they may treat one number as an object and use the process embedded in the other to increment in ones. Though usually shorter than count-all, count-on remains a counting process which takes place in time. By using it a child may be able to compute the result without necessarily linking input and output in a form that will be remembered as a new fact. Some children – often with a limited array of known facts – may become so efficient in counting, that they use it as a universal method that does not involve them in the risk of attempting to use a limited number of known facts. However, count-on may lead to development of a procept. It can produce a result that is seen both as a counting procedure and a number concept.

The proceptual divide

In the early stages, number is widely seen as a counting process. It is only when the child realizes that the number of elements is independent of the way in which the elements are arranged and of the order in which they are counted, that number can begin to take on its own stable existence as a mental object. During Key Stage 1, most children count at least some of the time, and some children count all the time. Those who count quickly can succeed in the number facts to 10 almost as well, and sometimes better, than those who know or can manipulate number facts. But those who achieve higher levels do so because they begin to see numbers as mental objects to be manipulated (Gray 1994). The more successful may still count, but they do so less and less, and when they do count, they use the technique sparingly in subtle ways (Thompson, Chapter 5, this volume), and thus are more likely to succeed than those that continue to count on a regular basis. The latter may develop intricate counting techniques using imaginary fingers, parts of the body, selected objects in the room, and so on, to cope with the number facts to twenty. But in doing so they give themselves a harder job to do than those who use number facts in a flexible way.

The divergence between those who interpret processes only as procedures and therefore make mathematics harder for themselves, and those that see them as flexible procepts, is called the 'proceptual divide' (Gray and Tall 1994). It is hypothesized that the difference between success and failure lies in the difference between the use of procepts and procedures. Those who use procedures where appropriate and symbols as manipulable objects where appropriate are said to be proceptual thinkers. It is further hypothesized that count-on is one procedure that causes a bifurcation between those who display the ability to think proceptually and those who think in terms of procedures (Gray 1993).

This divide between success and failure is found throughout the mathematics curriculum. At any stage, if the cognitive demands on the individual grow too great, it may be that someone, previously successful, founders. Like Joseph, they may ask 'tell me how to do it', anxiously seeking the security of a procedure rather than the flexibility of procept. From this point on, failure is almost inevitable. It is for this reason that mathematics is known chiefly as a subject in which people fail, fail badly, and fail often.

Implications for teaching and learning

If number is seen as a flexible procept, evoking a mental object, or a counting process, whichever is the more fruitful at the time, then children are likely to build up known facts in a meaningful way. Thus the 'fact' that 4 + 3 is 7 becomes a flexible way of interchanging the notation 4 + 3 for the number 7. If 4 is taken from 7, then this number triple tells us that the number 3 remains. In this way, seeing addition as a flexible procept leads to subtraction being viewed as another way of formulating addition. Successful children learn how to derive new facts from old in a flexible way.

It helps us to realize that what we need to do is to help all children achieve the flexible form of thinking developed through compressing number processes into concepts. But at its highest level, such flexibility is only achieved if children also know number facts and number tables. Too frequently, for some children, counting becomes the focus of attention. This can make it very difficult to compress the number processes into an object. We not only need to provide all children with opportunities to think about the power and flexibility of the symbolism, but for some we need to give opportunities which may help them to make necessary links between combination and output without the use of a lengthy procedure. One method may be to give the child a calculator at the appropriate time. Of course, this in itself will not help children learn number facts, but it would help them to relate similar problems and observe the patterns. With a 'supercalculator', a calculator which has the potential for a graphical display, a child may see on display at the same time not only the fact that 3 + 4 is equal to 7 but also that 4 + 3 is 7, 2 + 5 is 7, 9 − 2 is 7, and so on. Because several combinations can be built and seen in sequence, a child can easily try 13 + 4, 23 + 4, and may begin to see a pattern. By providing the supercalculator, we not only give an alternative representation for the numbers but we also provide an alternative way to deal with them. We offer a 'button-pressing' procedure which permits the child to see a representation which includes inputs and outputs without lengthy counting procedures mitigating against their connection. In such a way, we may help the child appreciate the pattern and develop some flexibility to solve harder combinations.

Will such a strategy improve all children's ability at arithmetic? In some senses there may be a problem. After all, if some children, because of their lack of success at arithmetic, turn to using procedures while we may want to make them flexible, it may be that the best we can do is to teach them procedures to make them flexible. In other words, we don't make them really flexible at all. Simply giving procedural children more examples to practise may help them in one way; it may make the procedures they use a little faster and perhaps a little more efficient, but in other ways it could be very damaging in that what they do without guidance is to develop their own idiosyncratic methods which in fact make the mathematics far harder. We therefore need to combine the practice of those facts which are essential building blocks in the system with the flexible means by which they can be manipulated most easily. This may mean practising number combinations so that they become automatic, but this must not set arithmetic in the context of something which *must* be learned by rote. Those who are successful at arithmetic have more than this. They use the facts they know to build the ones they don't know. They see the arithmetical symbol in a flexible way: it is both a process which enables them to do mathematics and a mental concept which enables them to think about it.

References

Baroody, A.J. and Ginsburg, H.P. (1986) The relationship between initial meaningful and mechanical knowledge of arithmetic. In J. Hiebert (ed.), *Conceptual and Procedural Knowledge: The Case for Mathematics*, pp. 75–112. Hillsdale, NJ: Lawrence Erlbaum Associates.

Fuson, K. and Fuson, A.M. (1992) Instruction supporting children's counting-on for addition and counting-up for subtraction. *Journal for Research in Mathematics Education*, 23(1): 52–78.

Gray, E.M. (1991) An analysis of diverging approaches to simple arithmetic: Preference and its consequences. *Educational Studies in Mathematics*, 22, 551–74.

Gray, E.M. (1993) Count-on: The parting of the ways in simple arithmetic. In I. Hirabayashi, N. Hohda, K. Shigematsu and Fou-Lai Lin (eds), *Proceedings of the XVII International Conference for the Psychology of Mathematics Education*, Vol. I, pp. 204–11. Tsukuba: Programme Committee.

Gray, E.M. (1994) Spectrums of performance in two digit addition and subtraction. In J.P. Ponte and J.F. Matos (eds), *Proceedings of the XVIII International Conference for the Psychology of Mathematics Education*, Vol. III, pp. 25–32. Lisbon: Programme Committee.

Gray, E.M. and Tall D.O. (1994) Duality, ambiguity and flexibility: A proceptual view of simple arithmetic. *Journal for Research in Mathematics Education*, 25(2): 115–14.

Steffe, L.P., von Glaserfeld, E., Richard, J. and Cobb, P. (1983) *Children's Counting Types: Philosophy, Theory and Application*. New York: Praeger Scientific.

Section 3

WRITTEN NUMBER WORK

Researchers have shown that young children begin to learn about the various written symbol systems, such as numerals and letters, some time before they start school, and construct meanings for written numerals observed in a variety of real-life contexts. On the other hand, schools often seem to rush into the introduction of formal standardized written algorithms far too early, leading to many children struggling to carry out half-remembered rules. Helping children to develop confidence in the use of written symbolism is an important, but difficult, aspect of a teacher's job. This section considers three different aspects associated with written representation.

Sue Gifford (Chapter 7) discusses the 'Emergent Maths' movement, describing its provenance and its relationship to a parallel movement in the development of children's literacy. She describes the British and Australian versions of this movement and discusses the strengths and weaknesses of their respective approaches. She compares her own research findings with those of other researchers in the field, and illustrates her argument with specific examples of children's work. She offers ideas for introducing young children to symbols in such a way that their experience and understanding are not limited.

In Chapter 8, Penny Munn suggests that there is a natural progression of rules for interpreting signs and making meaning in the area of language, and questions whether a similar progression exists in the area of number. She describes a small-scale research experiment which provided data suitable for the formulation of a possible answer to this question. She found that those children who used their own idiosyncratic notation to describe the contents of several tins were not as successful as those who used conventional numerals when it came to deciding which tin had had an extra brick added. She concludes that in situations where children are expected to use their mathematical writing to communicate quantity, the conventional system of numerals is more useful than self-invented notation.

The feasibility of helping children to develop written calculation methods which reflect their own mental methods is the focus of Chapter 9 by Ian

Thompson. He considers some of the research dealing with young children's use of mathematical symbolism, and discusses the differences between mental and written algorithms. Various strategies for carrying out the mental addition of two-digit numbers are analysed, and these are compared with the written algorithms produced by classes of children who had not been taught standard methods of computation. He suggests that the 'user-friendly' algorithms that some children invent for themselves fall into identifiable categories, and concludes that, provided teachers spend a substantial amount of time developing their children's mental calculation skills and making themselves aware of each child's preferred way of working, it is possible to help them develop written methods that do reflect their mental methods.

'When should they start doing sums?' A critical consideration of the 'emergent mathematics' approach

Sue Gifford

Introduction

'When should they start doing sums?' I was asked this question recently by a reception teacher who has thirty-five 4- and 5-year-olds in a small class-room. She had been doing lots of games, rhymes and practical problem-solving with the children, and some of them were now 'number experts'. I knew there was pressure to do sums from the parents and from the Year 1 teacher, too. I also knew that giving some children sums would ease the problem of managing the thirty-five in a confined space.

However, this teacher knows that young children can be taught to do sums like $3 + 2 = ?$ too soon, by just memorizing a procedure. This means they can read the numerals and count cubes, but have no understanding of addition and no idea of combining numbers to make other numbers. They cannot explain what they are doing or why, and have no alternative strat-egies which they could apply to addition problems set in a context. They would certainly not be able to relate the plus and equals signs to other problems. However, said the teacher, if some children could solve practical addition and subtraction problems, if they could justify their methods and predict the outcomes, as some of her 4-year-olds could, where is the harm in them doing sums and using the symbols? Surely our aim is to get children to think in more abstract ways? If they were not ready yet, how would she be able to tell when they were?

My initial reaction was to think that sums are inappropriate for 4-year-olds, who should really be in a nursery class. I replied that the children should be playing more games, solving a greater variety of problems, real and imaginary, and developing mental strategies for addition and subtrac-tion. If they were into more focused work, they should be investigating different ways of splitting up numbers in a variety of contexts. There were plenty of other aspects of number they could be developing, such as comparing, estimating, and counting larger numbers. They could talk about what they were doing, record in their own way, and play with calculators.

However, I felt a bit uneasy about this, my stock reply. Was there not an emotional element in it, influenced by Victorian images of young children sitting in rows doing sums? Was I not just passing on the received dogma of mathematics educationists: 'Thou shalt not do sums with little children'? I know that doing sums by counting cubes can encourage a reliance on counting strategies, rather than developing more effective mental strategies. I know that even the SCAA pre-school *Desirable Outcomes* (1996) advocates discussion of practical addition and subtraction activities, rather than recording in sum form. But I also know that young children can deal with abstract number symbols and mental problems. I usually argue that we should raise our expectations of what young children can do and stop thinking in terms of 'readiness', or ages and stages. So why should these 'number experts' not do sums just because they are 4? So long as they felt confident and unpressured, was I really convinced that it was wrong for them to do some sums?

The approach which I have been advocating for the past few years (Gifford 1990) might be categorized as typical of that of the emergent mathematics movement. This suggests that children start from practical activities and represent these in their own personal ways, gradually adopting standard written forms. This is in contrast to children doing sums or filling in worksheets, where they are starting from the written record, following instructions and trying to interpret someone else's way of recording. However, perhaps it was time for me to question this approach. In my experience, children's own representations of practical mathematical activities are not very common, and emergent mathematics in this sense has not made much impact on classrooms in general. One reason for this must be that, in class management terms, it seems easier to give children written tasks and to structure their recording.

The question is, does an emergent approach to written mathematics really help children in the development of their understanding of operations and symbols?

What is emergent mathematics and where does it come from?

Atkinson (1992) charts the derivation of this approach from psychological research and its influence on literacy teaching. Mathematics education has remained relatively unaffected by the work of Vygotsky (1978), whereas literacy education has taken on Vygotsky's emphasis on the child as an active learner in a social context, acquiring 'cultural tools' like language and symbolization through collaborative problem-solving with experts. According to Vygotsky, children can learn to use symbols from an early age, but they learn because they have real purposes for communicating in everyday social contexts.

One effect of this work has been to consider young children as learners in a more positive light, and this has been emphasized by language and literacy educators. Hall (1987), writing about emergent literacy, describes the change of emphasis from seeing children as competent rather than incompetent, as 'half full rather than half empty'. For instance, in language research, children's errors, like saying 'mouses' instead of mice, have come to be seen as the result of applying logical strategies and attempting to make sense, rather than as signs of confusion. The emergent literacy movement builds on a range of accounts of young children's spontaneous efforts to read and write before formal instruction in school.

The main implication of this view is that children do not need sequenced learning programmes of simplified skills. Purposes are the key: according to Vygotsky (1978), 'Reading and writing must be something the child needs'. The role of the adult is therefore mainly to provide purposeful contexts and audiences and to be the supportive expert. With literacy learning this means encouraging children to read books for pleasure and information, and to write in order to communicate with a responsive audience, for instance by writing stories which are 'published' within the classroom or school. Beyond this, the role of the teacher is in danger of being seen as *laissez-faire*, waiting for children's literacy to emerge naturally. However, a Vygotskian model implies an active role for the teacher as expert helper, sharing their knowledge and modelling literacy processes. 'Shared writing' is one example of this, where a teacher talks through the processes of composition and spelling. Vygotsky's idea of the 'Zone of Proximal Development' (where what children can do with help today, shows what they will be able to do on their own tomorrow) also implies an assessment and instructional role for the teacher in identifying what to help the child learn next.

Emergent mathematics draws on possible parallels between learning literacy and mathematics, and has different versions in Britain and in Australia, where the emergent literacy approach had a strong following.

The British model of emergent mathematics

Whitebread (1995) defined emergent mathematics by identifying four themes:

- placing tasks in meaningful contexts;
- requiring children to make their own representations;
- encouraging and developing children's strategies;
- employing a style of teaching which focuses on processes rather than products.

He describes an approach which results from research into children's early learning, and which, like emergent literacy, builds on pre-school experience and values informal strategies. This is to bridge the gulf between home and school mathematics, as described by such researchers as Hughes (1986). The fourth point involves an emphasis on discussion and reflection on processes or metacognition, with reference to Vygotsky.

Atkinson (1992) outlines a similar approach as 'mathematics with reason'. (Atkinson rejects the label 'emergent mathematics' presumably because of the connotations of a *laissez-faire* teacher role.) Her twelve identifying features may be summarized as seeing:

- children as actively making sense of experience, with their own methods and strategies, and bringing with them 'home learning';
- mathematics primarily as processes, valued because of 'its power to communicate and explain', rooted in the real world;
- the teacher's role as providing problem-solving activities derived from everyday situations, developing discussion, mental images and understanding through activity, encouraging positive attitudes with acceptance of individual methods and encouraging risk taking.

The parallels with emergent literacy, and influence from Vygotsky, may be clearly seen in both of these versions in their emphasis on meaningful contexts, discussion of processes, and valuing children's own methods. However, whereas Whitebread is concerned with emergent *written* mathematics, through children's own representations, Atkinson emphasizes *mental images*, implying that there is not such a direct relationship between written mathematics and literacy. This also reflects current concerns with mental mathematics, as considered elsewhere in this book.

The Australian model

Australian writers such as Stoessinger and Wilkinson (1991) have put more emphasis on children's written mathematics as a process of personal invention and approximation, building on primary teachers' greater confidence with literacy teaching using an emergent approach. Stoessinger discusses the difficulties of too close a parallel: he is not just concerned with emergent written mathematics, or a Vygotskian view of socially relevant mathematics. The parallel is with 'what real mathematicians do' and he describes children 'engaging with major mathematical ideas' through open-ended and challenging activities.

Stoessinger and Wilkinson (1991) also counter a *laissez-faire* image of the teacher's role, arguing that teachers are continually assessing and providing suitably challenging activities, demonstrating standard forms and 'asking questions which may prompt the student to clarify, to predict, to develop further, to look for alternatives'. Various principles from emergent literacy are used by the Australian model, which emphasizes the role of audiences for mathematical writing, and refers to 'publishing' children's mathematical theories within the classroom, by providing feedback times, noticeboards, or taking reports to other classes. Also important is the idea of 'immersion' in a rich mathematical environment, with children exposed to ideas beyond their understanding in an unpressurized way, just as they are exposed to print from an early age.

The Australian model of emergent mathematics therefore provides a clearer image of the teacher's role in terms of activities and support for children's learning.

What is the problem with young children using sums?

To return to the original question of young children doing sums, why is an emergent approach to written mathematics preferable? One concern is that children see plus and minus signs merely as prompts to count bricks or fingers, without any understanding of them as symbols representing the operations of addition and subtraction. Hughes (1986) investigated this by seeing whether children could use symbols to record practical examples of addition and subtraction. Of ninety children aged 3–7 years, most of whom were used to doing sums, none used addition and subtraction signs to record the activities. Hughes concluded that, 'the whole notion of representing these transformations on paper is something which children find very hard to grasp, although the exact reason for this difficulty is not yet entirely clear', and that there is 'a universal reluctance to use the symbols of school arithmetic'.

However, from my own experience, Hughes's results are not typical. In a previous account (Gifford 1990), I described young children recording practical addition and subtraction activities in their own ways, not only using a range of forms, including pictures, written words, numbers, but also plus and minus signs. In group situations, once one child had thought to use symbols, the others usually followed with alacrity rather than 'universal reluctance'. The children I was working with at the time were involved in the CAN project, and had not been used to plus and minus signs, except on the calculator.

The key activity to focus children on operations seemed to me to be the practical function machine, where children guess what operation the machine is performing. They choose a number of cubes to put in one side of the machine, the machine operator secretly adds some or takes some away, according to a rule, and pushes the resulting number of cubes out of the other side of the machine. The children have to guess the rule, which is written as a secret instruction for the machine operator to follow. This activity seems to be consistent with an emergent mathematics approach in providing a clear purpose and audience for mathematical communication. If children have small pieces of paper, it also encourages them to use abbreviated forms and symbols. This activity, I find, typically results in Year 2 children writing numbers and abbreviations of words, such as '4m' for 4 more, until someone thinks of plus and minus signs, and then they all use those (Fig. 7.1).

There are various possible explanations for the difference between my findings and those of Hughes. The lack of experience of sums may be one, although one child who used this form of recording had experience of sums from her previous school. Perhaps the experience with the calculator made

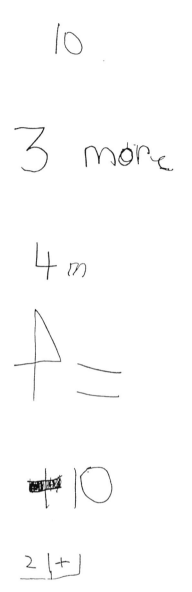

Figure 7.1 Children's instructions to the function machine operator

them more aware of using signs on keys to perform operations related to a variety of problems. Perhaps they were more used to recording in their own way and felt less pressured with a familiar person. The children knew me as a 'maths person', and this therefore suggested to them that mathematical symbols might be appropriate. I wondered if Hughes's children assumed that drawings were required because he had not suggested symbols were a possibility (or because of the quality of paper and pens supplied!) The children's 'reluctance' to use signs might be more to do with their attempts to guess what the adult wanted, rather than an inability to use them. A fairer assessment of children's ability to use symbolic recording might be to suggest to them that they could use symbols if they wanted to.

I decided to ask a small group of 4- and 5-year-olds to record some practical addition and subtraction problems, letting them do this in their own way in the first instance, but then prompting them to write 'sums' if they could. These children had previously been presented with addition sums on cards as part of a mental maths game, and they had no experience of minus signs from school. The activity was related to Hughes's box game: there were, say, three plastic bears under a pot, and I either slipped two out or added two, so that the children could not see how many were under the pot. After the children had successfully calculated the answer, I asked them to record, as Hughes had, by asking, 'Could you put something on the paper to show that we had three and added two more?' (or that 'we had three and took two away?').

These were confident 4- and 5-year-olds from relatively advantaged backgrounds. Nevertheless, I was surprised that out of six children, five used plus signs to record this new activity and perhaps even more surprisingly, they used abstract language to talk about what they were doing. As I expected, one child (Laura-Jayne) needed prompting to use the symbols (Fig. 7.2):

L-J.:	[8 – 4 from pot – responds instantly] 4
S.G.:	How did you know?
L-J.:	Because 4 and 4 is 8.
	[8 – 3: uses fingers] 5
	[2 + 3] Ooh hardy-wardy! [uses fingers] Two plus three is five.
S.G.:	Can you put something on the paper to show that we had 2 and added 3?
L-J.:	[Draws pot, then table, then bears]
Another child:	What's she doing?
L-J.:	Drawing teddy bears, adding some together
	[Draws 2 bears] I'm gonna do a hand putting them in.
S.G.:	Does this show that we had 2 and added 3 more?
L-J.:	You've got some in your hand
	[Draws 3 bears with one in the hand]
S.G.:	What can we do to show that we had 2 and added 3 more?
L-J.:	We could write 'We had 2 and added 3'.
S.G.:	Can you write a sum to show that we had 2 and added 3 more?
L-J.:	[Writes] 2 + 3 [pause] = 5
	It goes the opposite way to a 2.
	[Matches plastic bears onto the drawn bears and draws an extra one on the left]

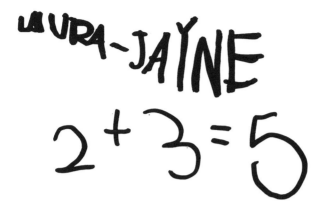

Figure 7.2 Laura-Jayne's representation of three bears under the pot with two more added

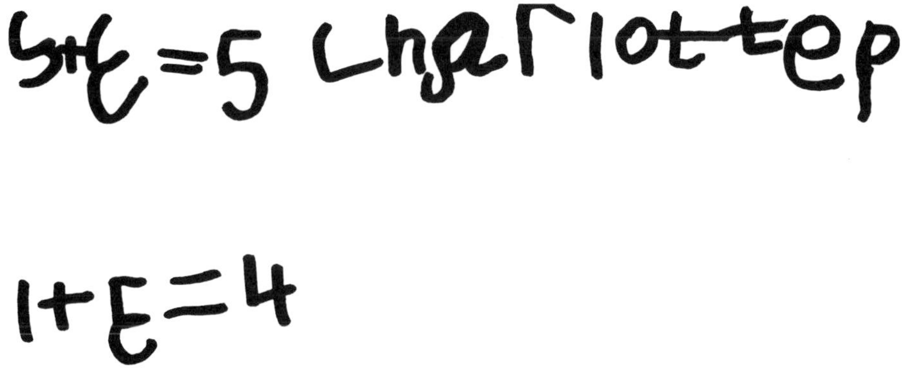

5+£=5 Lhɑɾʅoʈʈeρ

1+£=4

Figure 7.3 Charlotte's record showing 'two add one' turned into a new sum

Laura-Jayne's response might have been misinterpreted as showing an inability to use symbols, had I not asked her to do a sum. Actually, she seems to have more difficulty in remembering which way round to do a five than in writing the sum. Because there was no mathematical purpose for the record or incentive to use economical recording forms, her response was full of contextual details and very unmathematical, ignoring the number of bears. However, she was not only able to write the sum, but also used abstract language and fingers to represent the problem.

Another child spontaneously wrote a sum, but not as a direct representation of the problem. Charlotte, in response to 'we had two and we added one', wrote 2 and the total 3, and then said:

You've got to have like this in the middle [writes + in between 2 and 3]. Then you've got to plus it [writes = 5]. [She now has 2 + 3 = 5 and reads it]: 2 plus 3 makes 5 (Fig. 7.3).

Charlotte recorded the activity without using signs, then spontaneously turned her two numbers into an abstract problem, which she then completed. She seems to see the equals sign as a prompt for adding, although she then reads it as 'makes'. She also seems interested in 'playing' with writing in the sum form.

Chantelle (Fig. 7.4) was also confident with using plus signs, and in writing sums unrelated to the practical activity:

S.G.: Can you put something on the paper to show that we had one and added 3 more?
C.: [Writes] 1 + 3
S.G.: Can you show that it makes 4?
C.: [Writes] 4+
S.G.: [After another calculation] We had 2 and added another 2.
C.: [Writes 2 + 2, with first 2 reversed]
S.G.: Can you show that altogether it makes 4?

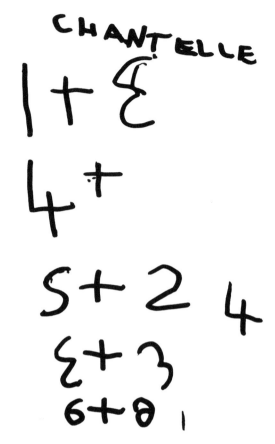

Figure 7.4 Chantelle's response to, and extension of, the 'add more' task

C.: [Thinks then writes] 4 [paper shows 2 + 2   4]
S.G.: [As she seems to be thinking] Are you thinking you want to put something else?
C.: Yes.
S.G.: What else do you want to put?
C.: Plus three plus four.
 [Writes 3 + 3, with first 3 reversed]
 Three plus three [counts the bits on the threes] six.
 [Writes 6 + 6, with last 6 reversed – this seems to be her way of recording the total, or she is stuck in the pattern of doubles].

It seemed that Chantelle was interested in making the numbers 'face' each other and in the visual symmetry of adding the same numbers. Like Charlotte, she was rehearsing her knowledge of the 'sum' form, rather than recording the practical activity. What these children seemed to respond to was the opportunity to *write* sums of their own, rather than to do sums as written tasks. This suggests parallels with emergent literacy, and the Vygotskian idea of children actively trying to make sense of symbol systems through experimenting. It also suggests that, although some children, and possibly those less advantaged than these, do have difficulties with signs, we should not have ceilings on our expectations of children due to their age.

One key factor here would seem to be the influence of the teacher in helping these children to relate the language and signs to practical situations. She has read sums to them and they have adopted this language and can apply it. They seem confident and willing to have a go, presumably as a result of unpressurized teaching. However, they are not very clear about equals and minus signs, which involve the more difficult concepts of 'equality' and subtraction. Whether the children could relate signs to other problem situations is another question, concerning the nature of the concepts represented by the signs.

The main problem, according to summaries of research such as that by Baroody and Standifer (1993), is that children have difficulty relating plus, minus and equals signs to all the different aspects of the concepts involved. For instance, they relate minus signs only to 'taking away' and not to 'difference' situations. Dickson *et al.* (1984) quote Tony, when faced with a 'How many more?' type subtraction saying, 'I don't know the sign for adding on'. Children tend to 'read' signs with one phrase, usually involving actions, like 'taking away', rather than relating them to relationships between numbers, such as comparisons. Like Charlotte, they see the equals sign as an operator, as a prompt to 'plus it', rather than as indicating equivalence between both sides of the equation. Clearly this is a potential danger of a narrow experience of sums where the minus sign is always read as an instruction to 'take away' cubes. The aim, as the National Curriculum Programme of Study for Key Stage 1 states (DfE 1995), is for children to relate 'mathematical symbols, e.g. '+', '=', to a range of situations' and this must involve a range of language too.

What are the advantages and disadvantages of an emergent approach? Implications for teaching and learning

One advantage of an emergent approach is the use of signs for recording practical problem situations. This enables the teacher to make links between different aspects of an operation, by showing that the same words and signs relate to a variety of contexts, thus preventing children giving limited meanings to signs. The practical to abstract progression is supported, as Whitebread points out, by Bruner (1966), who proposed that there were three stages in representing ideas: the enactive, the iconic and the symbolic. This is usually interpreted as involving apparatus, followed by pictorial then symbolic representation, and is a commonly recommended approach. There are, however, problems with this theory: Bruner included words as symbols in the third stage, whereas usually teachers see language as accompanying all stages of the process. Pictorial representations may be suitable for representing amounts, but unhelpful for representing operations. Dufour Janvier *et al.* (1987) argue that these are better represented through language, as the children using the function machine did when writing '4m' for '4 more'.

It may therefore be more useful for children to record operations using abbreviated words than using pictures, making an easier transition to symbols. Another issue with this progression is that learning may not be that tidy in reality: children may learn abstract forms first, from experience out of school, then relate them to practical situations. For instance, children may do sums with older siblings or use plus and minus signs to alter video channels. We may need to acknowledge this and to offer children opportunities to play at using abstract forms, as with a new 'genre' of writing. An emergent approach allows for this kind of flexibility.

The advantage of an emergent approach in encouraging children's own representations, is that it allows children to make sense of ideas by representing them in their own way. This then allows teachers to assess and build on children's thinking and prevents the inappropriate imposition of images on their thinking. Since we do not know exactly how visual images or words help children form concepts of operations, taking cues from children's recordings can help with this. For instance, Koysor's record of finding the difference between numbers on the number line, showed that she was thinking in terms of distance to represent the greatest difference (Fig. 7.5). This is an image which her teacher could then develop.

However, there is little or no research evidence to suggest that letting children record in their own ways actually enables children to understand operations better. The CAN project, which encouraged children to use calculators and to record in their own ways, reported that children gradually came to adopt the standard forms of recording with understanding. It is interesting to note that some of the newer published schemes for mathematics do encourage children's own recording and that the National Curriculum requires children to record 'in a variety of ways including ways which relate to their mental work': presumably these, like mental strategies, may be idiosyncratic, individual and 'emergent'. Another argument against an emergent approach is that teachers may waste time waiting for children to 'discover' more efficient standard forms. While children may choose how they record, teachers certainly need to demonstrate the use of signs and to encourage children to use them.

Another danger is of a lack of direction from the teacher in avoiding misconceptions. The alternative is to tackle these directly, by offering children choices which include possible misconceptions and by asking them to justify their choices. Baroody and Standifer (1993) give a useful summary of these kinds of activities; which include giving children sums on cards to match to practical situations, as suggested in rich variety by Barratta Lorton (1976). One advantage of these activities is that young children do not have to physically record, making it easier for them to focus on the meanings for symbols.

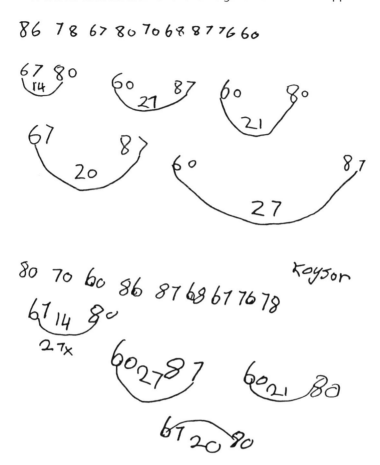

Figure 7.5 Koysor's idiosyncratic notation for finding the largest difference between pairs of numbers

Other activities include selecting the 'sum' with the correct operation to match a verbal problem, and matching a range of words and phrases to a sign. Alternatively, children are asked to make up a range of stories to match a sum. They may complete 'number sentences' in a variety of forms, including those which are less common, such as 10 = ? + ?. Using an equalizer balance seems helpful in establishing the equivalence meaning of the 'equals' sign. Using the calculator to select the correct operation to solve a problem is important as a life skill; children who know they can solve 'how many more?' type problems using the minus key are well on the way to having a broad concept of subtraction.

In conclusion, while it seems more effective for teachers to directly address possible misconceptions about symbols, emergent mathematics seems to have distinct advantages in encouraging children to make sense of written mathematics. Sums, when used to present tasks to children, are in danger of limiting children's experience and understanding. If teachers help children to relate a wide range of problems and language to written arithmetic, and allow them to write mathematics in ways they understand, then there is more chance of them being able to apply abstract symbols flexibly. Chidren's own representations also give us more clues as to how children are thinking mathematically. Given the need for teachers to place more emphasis on mental mathematics, this may be the real advantage of an emergent mathematics approach.

Acknowledgements

The author wishes to thank the children and staff of All Saints C.E. Primary School, Carshalton, and Colluden Primary School, Tower Hamlets.

References

Atkinson, S. (1992) *Mathematics with Reason*. London: Hodder and Stoughton.
Baroody, A. and Standifer, D.J. (1993) Addition and subtraction in the primary grades. In R.J. Jensen (ed.), *Research Ideas for the Classroom: Early Childhood Mathematics*, pp. 72–102. New York: Macmillan.
Barratta Lorton, M. (1976) *Workjobs 2*. Menlo Park, CA: Addison-Wesley.
Bruner, J. (1966) *Towards a Theory of Instruction*. Cambridge, MA: Harvard University Press.
Department for the Environment (1995) *Mathematics in the National Curriculum*. London: HMSO.
Dickson, L., Brown, M. and Gibson, O. (1984) *Children Learning Mathematics*. London: Holt, Rinehart and Winston.
Dufour-Janvier, B., Bednarz, N. and Belanger, M. (1987) Pedagogical considerations concerning the problem of representation. In C. Janvier (ed.), *Problems of Representation in the Teaching and Learning of Mathematics*, pp. 109–22. Hillsdale, NJ: Lawrence Erlbaum Associates.
Gifford, S. (1990) Young children's representations of number operations. *Mathematics Teaching*, 132: 64–71.
Hall, N. (1987) *The Emergence of Literacy*. London: Hodder and Stoughton.
Hughes, M. (1986) *Children and Number*. Oxford: Blackwell.
SCAA (1996) *Desirable Outcomes for Children's Learning on Entering Compulsory Education*. London: SCAA.
Stoessinger, R. and Wilkinson, M. (1991) Emergent mathematics. *Education 3–13*, 19(1): 3–11.
Vygotsky, L. (1978) *Mind in Society*. Cambridge, MA: Harvard University Press.
Whitebread, D. (1995) Emergent mathematics. In J. Anghileri (ed.), *Children's Mathematical Thinking in the Primary Years*, pp. 11–40. London: Cassell.

Writing and number

Penny Munn

Introduction

Some infant and primary schools are beginning to wonder whether an 'emergent writing' programme will extend to the creation of an 'emergent numeracy' programme. This raises the question of whether emergent literacy is analogous to emergent numeracy. This chapter will attempt to define the link between writing and number in the early years. Emergent literacy schemes usually work within the framework of a progression from drawing to scribble writing to letters that 'stand' for words, letters that 'stand' for syllables and finally mature writing consisting of letters that stand for sounds. This progression is based on the view that, if we regard a variety of marks that can be read in different ways as signs, then even pre-literate children have experience of reading signs. The goal of emergent literacy schemes is to capitalize on this early experience. It is the relation between sign and referent that forms the basis of a progressive categorization of signs.

The most basic signs are those that have a causal relationship with what they indicate (footprints, for example, indicating someone's presence). The next category of signs consists of those that have a resemblance to what they indicate (drawings and pictures, for instance). The final category consists of symbols that are quite arbitrary in the way they encode meaning. The meaning cannot be derived from the symbol itself; some access must be had to the social rule that governs the relation. Drawings occupy an intermediate position in this categorization, since they both resemble the thing they signify and they also draw on the arbitrary symbolism prescribed by cultural convention. From the earliest stage in drawing people, children draw neither what they see nor what they know – they draw what they know others will understand. This early communicative aspect to drawing has long been exploited by therapists who interpret children's drawings as communication about un-spoken emotional states (see Koppitz 1968).

It may be valid in the realm of writing and language to assert a seam-less continuity between language, drawing, writing and reading. In this sphere very young children work with the knowledge that someone will understand them – that both their speech and their mark-making is com-municative. Emergent writing programmes capitalize on this early com-munication via signs and use it to help children understand those features of writing that communicate meaning to others. These early mark-making activities are used as a bridge to understanding the complicated letter–sound correspondences that constitute the basic rules for creating meaning with written symbols.

In the area of language, then, there is a natural progression of rules for interpreting signs and making meaning. What evidence is there that there is a similar progression from sign to symbol in the area of number? Are we justified in describing 'emergent numeracy' as analogous to 'emergent lit-eracy'? To explain some of the origins of 'emergent numeracy', I shall briefly describe Hughes's (1986) findings on how children represent number in written form. I shall then describe some of my own observations of develop-ments in pre-schoolers' written representations of number.

Children's written representations of number

Hughes's (1986) work was in part aimed at understanding children's puz-zling inability to transfer between the concrete level of manipulations on number and the symbolic level of written numerals. It is a phenomenon that has been frequently commented on and is a particular feature of children who are unschooled, or who have difficulties with arithmetic (Ginsburg 1977; Carraher *et al.* 1987). The phenomenon is that children may show the ability to add numbers higher than ten when dealing with blocks or coins but seem to lose it in the transfer to symbolic notation. Hughes's aim was to understand the transition from concrete to symbolic numerical representa-tion by tracing the early development of written number.

He invented a simple game in which children first played at hiding vari-ous amounts of objects inside tins and then labelled these tins with marks denoting the number of objects inside. The purpose of the labelling was 'to remember how many were inside' at a later time. Hughes found that very young children seemed to have a natural propensity to draw the quantities that they wanted to remember. They tended to use primitive tally systems that had a direct resemblance to the quantity that they wanted to remember. Children labelling the quantity 'four', for instance, would either make four tally strokes on the paper:

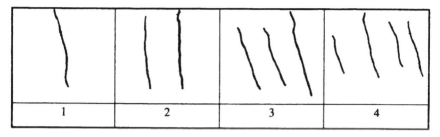

Figure 8.1 Quantities depicted by tally-marks

or they would construct an even more vivid depiction of the four blocks:

ℓ	**bO**	**Ø O₀ ◦**	**ØOØO**
1	2	3	4

Figure 8.2 Quantities depicted by pictograms

Hughes and his colleagues found that most children adopted these direct visual systems of recording before they started to use the conventional numerals. Use of numerals began with formal schooling and gradually eclipsed the more primitive 'iconic' labelling systems.

On the face of it, this trend seems to provide evidence for a developmental stage in which children invent systems of numerical notation for themselves. The analogy with emergent writing, where children bring their own meanings to communicative mark-making, seems convincing. However, there is a possibility that this bears only a surface resemblance to the way children's writing is rooted in lower-level systems of representation. The depth of the analogy depends on the children's understanding of their numeric mark-making as communicative and it is not clear from the data that they understood their activity to be communicative. If emergent number and emergent writing were truly similar, then this understanding would be present, because an understanding that symbols communicate meaning is a central element in the progression. Children's drawing is a precursor to writing because they believe that it can communicate ideas to other people. Although children were using marks to encode quantity in Hughes's study, there is little information on what the children thought their self-invented systems of notation communicated, either to themselves or to others. One child is cited as going to his labelled tin the following day and correctly predicting the quantity of objects within. However, there was no systematic exploration of this aspect of the children's mark-making. If we are to compare early numeracy with emergent writing, then we need to explore what the children understood their marks to communicate when they labelled their tins.

Do children understand that numeric notation communicates quantity?

To address this question, I shall describe my observations of the development of young children's written representations of quantity. The data come from the same longitudinal study described in Chapter 1. In another part of the number interview, I probed children's ways of writing quantity and their responses to what they had written. I adopted Hughes's 'tins' game, adding an extra turn designed to make the children read back the labels they had written so as to determine a quantity. I used four identical tins with hinged lids and small pieces of card as labels for the tins. With the tins open and containing respectively one, two, three and four blocks, I asked the children to 'write down how many blocks are in that tin'. I started at one and then went on systematically to four unless the child refused to attempt to write a quantity.

Not surprisingly, the responses I got from the children were similar to those given by Hughes's sample from the east coast of Scotland. Initially, the children drew pictograms or tallies to represent the number of blocks and only gradually developed the ability to symbolize the quantities using conventional numerals (for a detailed description, see Munn 1994). However, this only told me that the children were capable of representing quantity; it gave no information about what the children thought their written notation communicated. To investigate this, I introduced a hiding game designed to show whether they knew their writing would convey information about the quantity hidden within the tin. The additional game was only played with children who had number concepts of at least two and only with children who had read back to me the quantities they had written on the tin labels. I showed the children an extra block picked up from the pile beside the four labelled tins and told them that if they covered their eyes the playful teddy bear (an indispensable accomplice) would hide the block in one of the tins. The block was always hidden in the tin with two blocks. The question was, would the children read the label they had written for 'two' and realize that the three blocks inside the tin meant that this was the tin with the hidden block? It seemed an easy enough game. All the children had to do was to 'read' what they had written for 'two', compare it with the 'not-two' inside the tin, and then conclude that something had been added to the labelled tin.

It didn't surprise me that many of the children had problems with this game, since concepts of writing often develop some time after children have begun to develop their own writing systems. What did surprise me was the close connection between success on this task and the children's use of numerals (rather than pictograms and tallies) to record quantity. On the face of it, the pictograms and tallies that many of the children used were no worse, and might have been better, as memory aids than the numerals. However, very few children used pictograms as a reference (i.e. compared the drawings with the contents of each tin and concluded that only the quantity in the 'two' tin had changed). Most of the children who had represented quantity in the form of drawings ignored the labels and searched for other sources of information, such as the teddy bear or myself, to solve the puzzle.

Several children looked closely at the two tins containing three blocks, clearly understanding that something was wrong with one of them, but not knowing how to tell just which one had been changed. The triumphant performance of the children who had written numerals as labels (however inaccurately these numerals were formed) was a distinct contrast. They immediately knew that '2' signified something different from the three blocks within the tin. (In the following, C = child and I = interviewer.)

Child using pictograms/tallies
I: Which tin did he hide it in then?
C: Is it this one? This one? This one?
I: Which one is it?
C: I don't know.
I: How could you find out which tin it's hidden in?
C: We could ask that Teddy.

Child using numerals
I: Which tin did he hide it in then?
C: That one there.
I: How did you know that?
C: Cos look – two there and three there [points to label and then blocks].

It is important to emphasize here the longitudinal nature of the data. If the reactions of two groups of children – one using numerals, the other using drawings – had been compared, then it might be that the numeral users were simply 'cleverer' than the drawing users. However, with a longitudinal design there is no such comparison of different groups – the entire group is compared with itself and there isn't really an issue about 'hidden' differences that might be affecting the comparison. The children gradually adopted the numerals – a change that corresponded with increased number knowledge – and then began to use their own writing as a reference to solve the little problem. In the intermediate stages, when children were still developing their use of conventional numerals, they did on occasion fail to read back their written numerals. By the final pre-school visit, however, the pattern was very clear. All those children who had learned how to write numerals responded to them as signs that communicated quantity. Most of the children who had not learned how to write numerals did not treat the marks they had made as communicative in the same way. At the final visit, when the children had been at school for nearly a term, only nine children didn't use numerals to write quantity. However, not all those children who had learned to write numerals between the pre-school and school visits had learned about their communicative function. At the school visit there were seven numeral-using children who didn't read back the numerals to solve the problem in the 'hiding' game. This was a strong contrast to the pre-school pattern, and suggests that there was something different about the conditions of learning in school.

What determines children's understanding of their number writing?

Why was it that in the pre-school, those children who had used numerals found it easy to read them back but those children who had used drawings did not? First, the task of reading a tally record to discover any difference between label and contents is remarkably similar to the counting tasks that young children traditionally fail. According to my argument in Chapter 1, it simply would not occur to these children to count the little drawings, count the blocks, and then compare the results. However, this does not explain why they didn't compare the label visually with the contents of the tin, an easy enough task where the quantities of two and three are concerned. The second point is that the children's self-invented notation based on drawing probably lacked a communicative context. When pre-school children learn to write numerals, their learning is set in the context of interaction that clearly conveys the quantitative meaning of these symbols. When children invent ways of depicting quantity based on drawing, this is not necessarily so. The pre-schoolers who drew squares or tallies to record number were unlikely to have had any conversations about the meaning of their activity simply because such activity has no widespread cultural meaning.

These two factors together can account for those children at the school visit who did not think of reading back their numerals to discover 'how many'. The mental activity of comparison and quantification is based on counting, so children with poor counting skills would be unable to make much sense of conventional numerals. The children who learnt the conventional notation relatively late would also be very unlikely to have had extensive conversations about the meaning of the symbols they were producing. While the children were in pre-school there was time for them to integrate their understanding of quantity, counting and written numerals. They were experiencing a slow-paced curriculum in which they themselves decided when they would adopt the written numeric conventions of their culture. As they puzzled over their memories of the shape and orientation of the numerals, they had plenty of time to coordinate their number knowledge with their numeral knowledge. The children integrated their knowledge of numerals as a written communicative device with their number concepts. Those children who entered school with weak concepts of number did not seem to have had the time to develop this integration between their concept of writing and their concept of number. The curriculum (SPMG) forced the pace of their learning by demanding that they learn the numerals along with the number concepts. The paradoxical consequence of this was that they developed a use of numerals that was unrelated to their knowledge of number.

Discussion

To return to our initial question of whether the analogy between 'emergent literacy' and 'emergent numeracy' is a useful one, there are two interlinked issues. The first is whether picture reading forms a basis for understanding that numeric symbols relate to quantity. The second is whether the progression from drawing to symbol in number notation is in any way like the progression from drawing things to writing words.

The first question is answered by the finding that counting knowledge and number concepts mediated children's understanding of their pictograms as a communicative device. There was a very significant pattern whereby children were unable to use their self-invented number writing communicatively because these symbols were not established communicatively and because the children didn't relate them to their number concepts. There is therefore not a direct analogy between a drawing's communication of linguistic meaning and a pictogram's communication of numeric meaning. Although pictograms and tallies might look like simple drawings of quantity, they did not function in that way for these children. Even these primitive-looking number symbols only seemed to acquire a communicative function if the children talked about them and integrated them with concepts of number and counting.

The question about the similarity in progression is related to the first issue but is slightly different, emphasizing as it does the way the symbols were used either in referential or numeric contexts. The data suggest that understanding the numeral system as a conventional system for communicating quantity provides a powerful tool for the development of number activity. Recall that the pre-schoolers who used numerals were still at the stage of not counting spontaneously to determine quantity (see Chapter 1). Yet their use of conventional numerals enabled them to make automatic and unerring comparisons between concrete quantities and symbolic representations of quantities. The quantities involved were small, and the evidence indirect, but nevertheless it suggests that numeral understanding – when integrated with the development of number concepts – can 'bootstrap' numeracy development in ways far superior to concrete number experience. There can therefore be little similarity between developments in children's understanding of numerals and their understanding of writing.

Conclusions and implications for teaching

This analysis of emergent numeracy and emergent writing carries some clear implications for the earliest teaching of number. These implications concern children's access to the numeral system, the relation between numerals and iconic records, and the interactive basis of teaching ways of writing quantity. The first implication is related to the notion of 'personal meaning', which may be misplaced in discussions of emergent numeracy. When the children were asked to use their writing to think numerically, the conventional numerals were far more useful to them than their self-invented notation. In the context of number thinking, the symbols with conventional meaning have more power than symbols with personal meaning. The direction for teaching that this finding gives is towards the importance of ensuring that all children have access to the numeral system and that this conventional system acquires a direct meaning for all children.

The second implication for teaching centres on the finding that the children's primitive, iconic systems of recording didn't necessarily carry meaning about quantity. This was true for only a few children; presumably, quite sophisticated number skills are required to draw numerical conclusions from such records. In this respect, pictograms are not very different from numerals. Even though they look more 'concrete', they need to be read just like any other symbol, and children with poor number concepts will find them no more easy to read than conventional numerals. Especially in the primary curriculum, pictograms are often seen as serving the same function as concrete arrays. They do not. They need to be read in the same way as any other symbol and pictograms should not be used as a clarification of written numerals, as they so often are both in school and pre-school. The third implication is that the interaction and communication that take place around writing are far more important than previously thought. Whether tally-marks or numerals are used to record quantity, adults should talk to children about their symbolization so that children can, through this discourse, link the signs they use to their concepts of quantity.

Acknowledgements

This study was supported by ESRC Grant L208252005 and was part of the ESRC programme 'Innovation and Change in Education'. Thanks are due to the pre-school centres who took part in the study and to Strathclyde Region Education Department for help and cooperation.

References

Carraher, T.N., Carraher, D.W. and Schliemann, A.D. (1987) Mathematics in the streets and in schools. *British Journal of Developmental Psychology*, 3: 21–9.
Ginsburg, H.P. (1977) *Children's Arithmetic: The Learning Process*. New York: Van Nostrand.
Hughes, M. (1986) *Children and Number*. Oxford: Blackwell.
Koppitz, E.M. (1968) *Psychological Evaluation of Children's Human Figure Drawings*. New York: Grune and Stratton.
Munn, P. (1994) The early development of literacy and numeracy skills. *European Early Childhood Education Research Journal*, 2(1): 5–18.

Mental and written algorithms: can the gap be bridged?

Ian Thompson

Introduction

The National Curriculum documents for Scotland and for England and Wales stress the importance of children being able to make connections between mental and written calculation methods. The Scottish National Guidelines, *Mathematics 5–14* (SOED 1991), state that:

> Pupils will be better able to calculate when the written procedures they use support flexible efficient mental methods. Such personal proficiency mentally, supported with pencil and paper, is an important aim of mathematical education.

In a similar vein, the English and Welsh equivalent document, *Mathematics in the National Curriculum* (DfE 1995), informs us that pupils should be given the opportunity to 'record in a variety of ways, including ways that relate to their mental work'.

A strong emphasis on the acquisition of a wide range of flexible mental strategies and, in particular, on extensions of these to develop a range of non-calculator calculation methods, can also be found in the latter document in the context of multiplication and multi-digit addition and subtraction at Key Stage 2 and beyond. 'Standard algorithms' for written calculation do not warrant a mention. There does appear, however, to be an implicit assumption in both documents that an obvious and natural relationship exists between mental calculation methods and standard written algorithms. As the personal experience of many teachers might suggest otherwise, this chapter will consider some of the research relating to this issue, with the focus limited in the main to the operation of addition.

Young children and mathematical symbols

Aubrey (Chapter 2, this volume) discusses the knowledge and experience that young children bring with them to school. By this time, they have begun to learn about the various written symbol systems, such as numerals and letters, and have constructed meanings for written numerals observed in a variety of contexts. However, because numbers found in the environment are usually used for measuring, grading, categorizing or labelling objects, children hardly ever meet situations in the real world in which written numerals are used in their cardinal sense. It is also the case that the numerals that they experience in environmental situations are nearly always in ready-made form. Rarely do they see their peers or their parents writing numerals for personal reasons – except, perhaps, for the occasional note left for the milkman! The existence of this 'limited apprenticeship' in written number – compared to that experienced in connection with the written word – has implications for children's appreciation of the appropriateness of writing numerals for their own personal use or for communication. It also has implications for those mathematics educators who are advocating an 'emergent mathematics' approach modelled on the 'emergent literacy' movement (see Gifford, Chapter 7, this volume).

Hughes (1986) conducted a simple experiment with young children between the ages of 3 years 4 months and 7 years 6 months. Several bricks were placed on a table and then a few more were added. The children were asked to show on paper that first they had three bricks and then two more were added. Even though some of the children were at school and had been using the conventional arithmetic symbols '+', '−' and '=' in their exercise books, not a single child actually used these symbols in response to the researcher's request. Hughes argued that the children did not feel that these symbols were particularly relevant to the problems they had been asked to solve. Other researchers have obtained different results, and Gifford (Chapter 7, this volume) offers an explanation for these differences.

Research would therefore seem to suggest that use of standard mathematical symbols is something that develops slowly in young children. They need to be exposed to the symbols, but not obliged to use them until they feel comfortable with them. In this country, we appear to be obsessed with written work in mathematics. It is as if no work has been done unless there is a written record to verify it. But calculation takes place in the mind. It is only written down for one or more of the following reasons: as a record of the mental activity involved; as a means of clarifying one's thinking; as a means of support for the individual doing the mathematical thinking; or as a means of communication to others. Consequently, all calculations for children in the first few years of schooling should ideally be done mentally, using whatever aids they feel they need – counters, bricks, fingers, etc. All single-digit calculations, whether written or not, have to be done practically or mentally: writing the sum down does not 'support' the mental method used, whatever the method. Setting the sum out in standard vertical format with one number underneath the other serves no useful purpose other than as preparation for later work with two- and three-digit numbers.

If one is investigating a possible relationship between mental and written algorithms, it would seem to make sense, therefore, to focus upon calculation with multi-digit numbers. This takes us out of the normal range of many children in their early years of schooling, but it is nevertheless important that teachers are aware of where their attempts to help their children record in their own way may well be leading.

Differences between mental and written algorithms

Structural differences

Plunkett (1979) gives an interesting theoretical account of the differences between mental algorithms and standard written algorithms when he compares them on ten different criteria. He argues that standard written algorithms are symbolic, automatic, contracted, efficient, analytic and generalizable, whereas mental algorithms are fleeting, variable, flexible, iconic, holistic and are usually not generalizable.

An alternative way of looking at the structural differences is to consider the algorithms in action. If we take as one example the sum 47 + 36, we find that use of the standard algorithm dictates that the numbers be set down thus:

```
  47
+36
───
```

and that the 'patter' to accompany the calculation runs something like this: 'Seven and six make thirteen . . . Put down the three and carry the one . . . Four and three is seven . . . Seven and one makes eight'. While this rigmarole is being performed, various digits are written down, and finally the number 83 appears in the designated place. Mental or oral methods of solution are obviously less standardized, but one common method used by young children to perform such a calculation is: '47 + 36 . . . Forty and thirty makes seventy . . . Seven and six makes thirteen . . . Seventy and thirteen makes eighty-three'. Other idiosyncratic mental algorithms can be found in Thompson (Chapter 5, this volume).

A key idea in distinguishing between mental and written methods concerns the notion of 'direction'. In the case of the standard written algorithm described above, the sum is set out vertically and is tackled from right to left, whereas in the mental version it is usually set out horizontally and the answer is calculated from left to right. Another more subtle 'direction' difference concerns the manner in which the numbers are treated during the solution. Despite the fact that numbers are always read from left to right, it so happens that the standard procedures for addition, subtraction and multiplication oblige us to work in the opposite direction. The standard algorithm for addition treats each number to be added as a collection of discrete digits, where those set out underneath each other in the same column have to be combined as if they were actually units digits. This leads us to say,

'Four and three makes seven and one more makes eight' part way through calculating 47 + 36, when we actually mean 'Forty and thirty makes seventy and ten more makes eighty'. Use of the standard written algorithm obliges the user to disregard the meaning that the individual digits possess by dint of their position in the number, and forces them to indulge in pure symbol manipulation.

Mental methods, on the other hand, almost always retain the place value meaning of the digits and remain true to the language used when the number is spoken. The number 43, which, of course, is read as 'forty-three', is treated as a 40 (forty) and a 3 (three), and the individual performing the calculation proceeds to add the tens together, then the units, and finally combines the two subtotals. Working from left to right also means that the initial stages of the calculation give you a useful first approximation to the answer.

Perceived status differences

A video sequence from an Open University mathematics education pro-gramme (PME 235) shows 12-year-old Dean from the remedial group in a com-prehensive school attempting some subtractions. He is asked to write down the problems, which are given to him verbally, and to explain his method of working as he carries out the calculations. In response to the following subtraction:

716
−598

Dean writes 118 starting from the left-hand side, and explains 'Five from seven leaves 200, but as it's 98 it's . . . 118'. I would guess that the missing stages in Dean's explanation might be 'as it's 98 it's only one hundred . . . plus the 2 . . . and the other 16 . . .'.

When asked to work out 311 take away 214 he writes:

311
−214

and then after a few seconds pause he puts 97 beneath the line, writing the 9 underneath the 2 and the 7 under the 1. Pressed to explain his answer, Dean says: 'If that was 11 it would be 100 dead . . . but there's 14 instead of 11 . . . that's 3. So you take 3 away from 100 . . . that's 97'.

Dean's teacher decides to give him a more difficult problem next, so he is asked to find 4015 take away 617, which he sets out in the following manner:

4015
−607

with the 6 incorrectly placed under the 4. He then proceeds to explain: 'I take 5 away from 7 . . . leaves 2 . . . 1 from nought you can't do so 1 from 10 leaves 9 . . . So that means you go over to the 6 . . . Cross the 6 out and put a 5. That puts a 1 on [the zero] . . . 1 away from 10 leaves 9 . . . Nought away from 5 leaves 5 . . . and 4 on its own [giving an answer of 4592]. Despite the fact that the size of his answer should tell him that it must be wrong, Dean is happy with what he has done. After all, he has applied the teacher-taught algorithm, so it must be correct!

Dean's work clearly illustrates one major difference between personal maths and school maths: the former you do in your head in any way that you like, and the latter you do on paper following certain rules that your teacher has explained to you (and that you have probably forgotten, as in this case). Given numbers he feels confident with, Dean can use his excellent understanding of place value to generate some fascinating idiosyncratic mental calculation strategies. But when faced with more awkward numbers, he slips into 'school maths' mode, incorrectly copying down the problem; subtracting the smaller digits from the larger; exchanging a hundred for ten tens on the bottom line; and ending up with an answer to a subtraction which is larger than the number he first started with.

In an interesting study that casts a different light on the mental/written issue, Davis and McKnight (1980) used a written test of basic algorithmic skills with a group of 9- and 10-year-olds. Each child's individual incorrect solutions were collected together, and personalized follow-up mental tests were produced. The children were tested without being aware that their papers were all different. Those who then succeeded in giving correct mental answers were later told that one version of their calculation was incorrect. When asked which they thought was the incorrect answer, they invariably chose the mental version. This would appear to reveal a great deal about the children's perceptions of the status of written methods compared to mental methods. It also says something about their level of confidence in their own mental strategies.

A variety of research projects and surveys carried out in the 1980s found that teenagers at school, adolescents at work and adults in daily life all avoided the use of standard methods, preferring to use 'back of an envelope methods'. They were also dismissive of these methods, despite the fact that they usually provided them with the correct answer. What we appear to have is a situation whereby young children, teenagers and adults undervalue their own idiosyncratic mental methods, while setting great store by those written methods that they have spent many hours practising throughout their school careers, methods which in reality they do not use. The 'hidden curriculum' of schools has succeeded in persuading these individuals that written methods are vastly superior to mental ones.

Mental calculation methods for multi-digit numbers

It is possible to identify three broad categories of mental strategy used in the solution of such problems which I propose to call 'cumulative sums', 'partial sums' and 'cumulo-partial sums'. These strategies are best explained diagramatically, and 56 + 38 will be used as an illustrative example in each case.

Cumulative sums

$$56 \xrightarrow{+30} 86 \xrightarrow{+8} 94$$

In this strategy, one number, usually the larger, is taken as the starting point and the tens of the second number are added on to this number, usually in one fell swoop (56 . . . 86) or occasionally in steps of ten (56 . . . 66 . . . 76 . . . 86 . . .). The units in the second number are then added by one of a variety of means: number bonds (86 + 8 = 94), adding an easier number (86 + 10 = 96, 96 − 2 = 94), or bridging-up-through ten (86 + 4 = 90, 90 + 4 = 94). The method of cumulative sums appears to be popular among adults, but research with pre-teenage children suggests that this strategy is not used very often by young children in Britain. In a study by Jones (1975), which involved eighty 10- to 11-year-olds, less than 4 per cent used this strategy. Schliemann (1988) asked twenty 9- to 13-year-old Brazilian children working as street vendors to mentally solve 216 additions, and reported that this particular strategy was used much less frequently than any other she observed. Her report includes an excellent example of the method in action:

[28 + 19]: 28 plus 19, let me see [*pause*] 28 plus 19 [*pause*] 40 [*pause*] 47. This one I took 10 from 19 and put it on 28. Then I took 2 from 9 and I had 40. There was 7 left, it makes 47.

In the Netherlands this strategy is formally taught to young children (Beishuizen 1993) using the 'empty numberline' as a model.

Partial sums

When using this particular method, the tens and the units are added separately, and in the most common version of this strategy, 56 + 38 would be calculated mentally in this manner:

50 + 30 = 80, 6 + 8 = 14, 80 + 14 = 94.

Some children use the commutative property (6 + 8 = 8 + 6) and add the units in reverse order starting with the larger number first, while a minority add the units before they deal with the tens. Occasionally, a child will add the fourteen as a ten and a four:

50 + 30 = 80, 6 + 8 = 14, 80 + 10 = 90, 90 + 4 = 94.

The partial sums strategy appears to be the most common mental strategy used by young children in Britain for the mental addition of two-digit numbers. Jones (1975) found that 82.5 per cent of his sample of 10- to 11-year-olds used some version of this calculation method.

Cumulo-partial sums

This strategy, as the name suggests, is a hybrid of the two calculation methods described above. The child initially adds the tens and then uses this sum as a starting point for a cumulative addition. A diagrammatic representation of this method for 56 + 38 might look like this:

$$50 + 30 = 80, \; 80 \xrightarrow{+6} 86 \xrightarrow{+8} 94.$$

Other children would put the eight rather than the six on to the eighty, as this is the larger of the two units digits:

$$50 + 30 = 80, \; 80 \xrightarrow{+8} 88 \xrightarrow{+6} 94.$$

In fact, the phrase 'put the eight on the eighty' is used quite often by young children, and succinctly captures the dynamic aspect of their mental addition. Some of these children might then proceed by partitioning the 6 into 2 + 4 and use their knowledge of complements in ten to build the 88 into 90, adding the final four to give 94. Fourteen per cent of Jones's (1975) sample used some version of this particular mental strategy.

Written calculation methods for multi-digit addition

To investigate the idiosyncratic written calculation strategies used for two-digit addition, it is necessary to work with older children. One problem with this is that the children have already received a substantial amount of exposure to standard algorithms by the time they reach Year 3 or 4. To avoid this problem, I worked with a sample of 117 Year 5 (American Grade 4) children from four schools involved in the Calculator Aware Number (CAN) Curriculum Project, an offshoot of the nationally funded PrIME Project which ran from 1985 to 1989. The basic principle underlying the philosophy of schools involved in this project was that children should have unrestricted access to calculators from Year 2 onwards, and that traditional pencil-and-paper algorithms should not be formally taught.

In the study (see Thompson 1994), the children were presented with word problems commensurate with their age and ability. They were informed that the key to the calculator cupboard had been lost and were asked to write down their solutions to the problems, setting out their working in such a way that a friend could understand their method. They were also told that it did not matter whether their answers were right or wrong, as I was more interested in learning about the methods that they had used.

I found that 71 per cent of the children set out all of their calculations horizontally, with 15 per cent setting them out vertically and the remaining 14 per cent using a mixture of the two different layouts. In addition to this, 85 per cent consistently worked from left to right and a further 4 per cent varied the direction in which they worked. It is of interest to note that this 85 per cent included a number of children who set their work out vertically, as if preparing to use the standard algorithm, but who then proceeded to calculate from left to right.

The most common written algorithm used by the children was the method of partial sums, a finding in keeping with Jones's (1975) results in the area of mental calculation. Kerry's lucid explanation of her written procedure

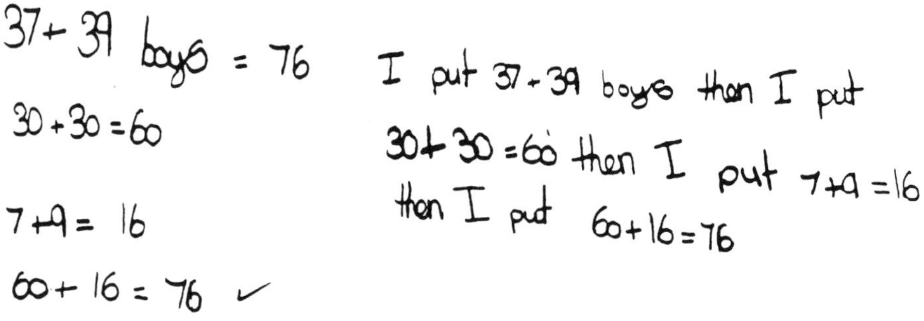

$$37 + 39 \text{ boys} = 76$$
$$30 + 30 = 60$$
$$7 + 9 = 16$$
$$60 + 16 = 76 \checkmark$$

I put 37 - 39 boys then I put
30 + 30 = 60 then I put 7 + 9 = 16
then I put 60 + 16 = 76

Figure 9.1 Kerry

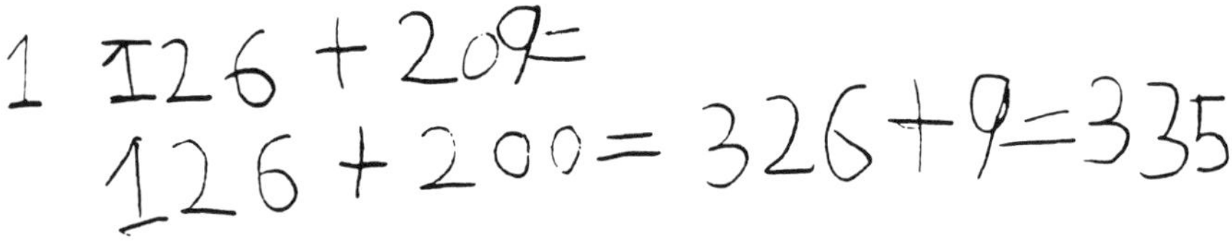

$$1 \quad 126 + 209 =$$
$$126 + 200 = 326 + 9 = 335$$

Figure 9.2 Marc

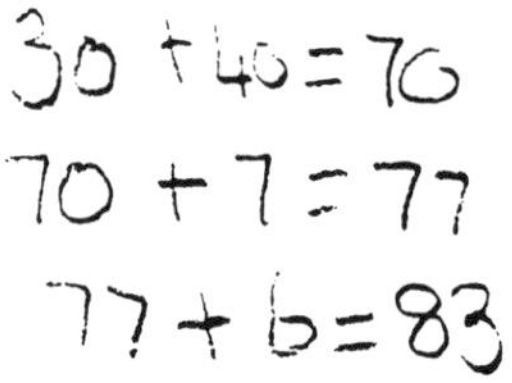

$$30 + 40 = 70$$
$$70 + 7 = 77$$
$$77 + 6 = 83$$

Figure 9.3 Michelle

(Fig. 9.1) constitutes an excellent example of this strategy. Only one of the 117 children involved in my study, Marc, used the method of cumulative sums favoured by many adults (Fig. 9.2). The third method, cumulo-partial sums, was used at some time by 28 per cent of the children, and Michelle's solution to 37 + 46 clearly illustrates the nature of this calculation method (Fig. 9.3).

Individual children in the study had developed slightly more formalized vertical algorithms. Denise's idiosyncratic layout of her problem (Fig. 9.4) provides an excellent example of an interesting invented notation, and also illustrates the extent to which the place value meaning of the digits has been maintained throughout her partial sums calculation. On the other hand, Emma appears to drop her cumulo-partial sums strategy part way through the calculation, as she does not write down the cumulative sub-total 69 (Fig. 9.5). Further questioning revealed that she had retained this in her head while adding on the remaining seven. She also explained that she 'took one

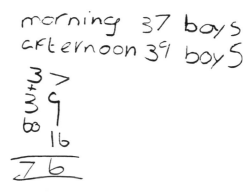

morning 37 boys
afternoon 39 boys

Figure 9.4 Denise

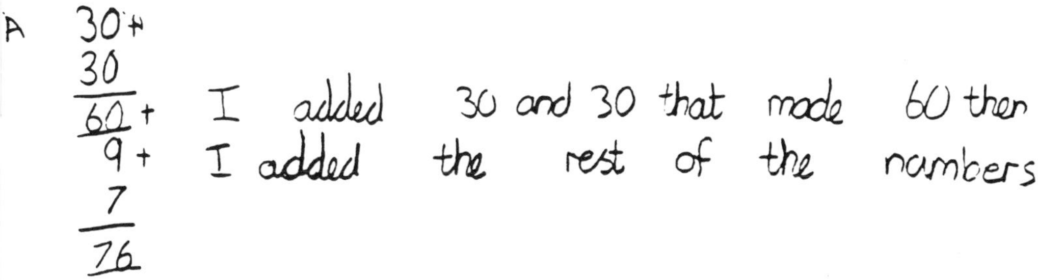

A

30 +
30
60 +   I added   30 and 30 that made   60 then
9 +   I added   the   rest   of   the   numbers
7
76

Figure 9.5 Emma

off to make 70, and so the answer was 76'. Emma is here making excellent use of the popular 'bridging-up-through-ten' mental calculation strategy discussed in the literature.

Implications for teaching

This discussion of relevant research suggests that it should be possible to achieve those aims set out in the National Curricula for Scotland and for England and Wales, which recommend that children's written methods should 'support' or 'relate to' their mental work. However, the strategies for achieving this are not as clear-cut as the relevant documents would appear to imply. Major changes in teachers' classroom practice are needed if these aims are to be achieved. One particular priority concerns the need for teachers to ensure that mental calculation is allocated a more prominent role in daily mathematical activities. The Non-Statutory Guidance (NCC 1989) states categorically that:

> The central place of mental methods should be reflected in an approach that encourages pupils to look at these methods as a *first resort* when a calculation is needed.

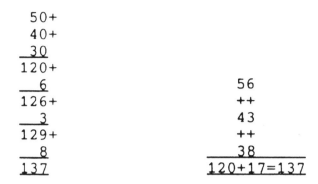

$$
\begin{array}{r}
50+ \\
40+ \\
\underline{30} \\
120+ \\
\underline{\ 6} \\
126+ \\
\underline{\ 3} \\
129+ \\
\underline{\ 8} \\
\underline{137}
\end{array}
\qquad
\begin{array}{r}
56 \\
++ \\
43 \\
++ \\
\underline{38} \\
\underline{120+17=137}
\end{array}
$$

Figure 9.6 Generalization of   *Figure 9.7* Generalization of
Emma's method   Denise's method

Bierhoff (1996) compared primary school mathematics textbooks in Britain with those used in Germany and Switzerland, supporting this comparison with observations of classroom practice in the three countries. Among the many differences noted by a team of mathematics educators was the important point – neglected in most of the newspaper reports at the time – that a much greater emphasis was placed on mental and oral calculation on the Continent. Teachers were also provided with a highly structured and detailed step-by-step teaching approach in the officially approved textbooks. One finding, which may well prove to be one of the most crucial in accounting for the apparent superior performance of Swiss and German 9-year-olds in international surveys, is succinctly expressed by Bierhoff (1996): 'Mental calculation is regarded on the Continent as a priority, to the exclusion of formal pencil and paper calculation until the age of nine'. This raises the question of whether British children's earlier start at school, given the inevitable formalizing of learning that this implies, actually works against them in this particular area of the curriculum.

Greater emphasis on mental and oral calculation would inevitably lead to more classroom discussion, both of the teacher–pupil and the pupil–pupil variety. This means that teachers would gain greater access to children's personal calculation strategies and thereby be in a better position to oversee the acquisition of related written algorithms.

Having ensured that substantial emphasis has been given to mental calculation and to the development of children's own methods of recording at Key Stage 1, some teachers of Years 4 and 5 may wish their children to develop more formalized or more structured procedures that bear a closer resemblance to the standard algorithm for addition. Those children who have a propensity towards using cumulo-partial sums methods could be guided to adopt the algorithm suggested in Fig. 9.6, which is a generalization of Emma's procedure. Other children who may prefer partial sums methods might feel more at ease with Denise's algorithm illustrated in Fig. 9.7. An interesting variation on both of these strategies is that of Kate (Fig. 9.8).

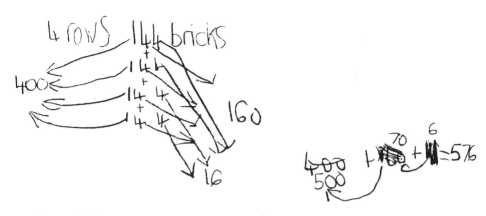

Figure 9.8 Kate

Kate has used a very elaborate but lucid algorithm for her calculation of the number of bricks in four rows given that there are 144 bricks in each row. Her idiosyncratic method shows very clearly the various stages in her thinking. She has set the numbers down underneath each other, even though all of her other work was in horizontal format, and has used arrows to explain to the reader how she has calculated the partial sums. The horizontal layout of the sums suggests that Kate has worked from left to right, and the crossings out and accompanying arrows illustrate the various regroupings that have been performed – one hundred has been transferred from the 160 to the 400, and ten has been transferred from the 16 to the 60. This regrouping has made the resulting addition (500 + 70 + 6) much simpler to perform. Kate would appear to have an excellent understanding of place value and a great deal of confidence in her own methods. Formalizing Kate's actual calculation gives a 'long' version of her algorithm (Fig. 9.9), and a 'short' version that could be adopted by those children who feel confident with the procedure (Fig. 9.10).

The advantages of these methods – either in idiosyncratic or formalized form – include the fact that the fundamental place value meaning of the numbers is retained, and this means that the children are manipulating quantities rather than symbols. The three methods also produce successive approximations to the answer, and are therefore more likely to provide useful cues as to the accuracy of the answer. Their main strength, however, lies in the fact that they model, more closely than does the standard algorithm for addition, the 'natural' mental calculation heuristics of many children. It is also of interest to note that none of the methods involves 'carrying' or 'putting milk bottles on doorsteps'!

To effect a realistic deployment of written methods that actually do reflect mental methods, children will need to be given greater encouragement to try out their own methods of calculation and to discuss and share these with their classmates. The teacher's task should be to ensure that opportunities are provided which might help stimulate this important discussion. Children

```
    144                          144
    144                          144
    144                          144
  +_144                        +_144
    400                          400
    160                          160
   _16                          _16
    500                          576
     70
    __6
    576
```

Figure 9.9 Generalization 1 of   *Figure 9.10* Generalization 2 of
Kate's method   Kate's method

will have to be praised for devising 'original' idiosyncratic procedures and encouraged to consider alternative ways of performing a given calculation. Teachers will also have to ensure that they do not formally teach the standard algorithms. They will need to use the available research and survey evidence to help them persuade parents that delaying written calculation methods is educationally sound. They will need to focus their attention on helping children to develop personal written algorithms which are efficient but which, more importantly, reflect both the children's own individual ways of construing number and their preferred methods of operating mentally with numbers.

References

Beishuizen, M. (1993) Mental strategies and materials or models for addition and subtraction up to 100 in Dutch second grades. *Journal for Research in Mathematics Education*, 24(4): 294–323.

Bierhoff, H. (1996) *Laying the Foundations of Numeracy: A Comparison of Primary Textbooks in Britain, Germany and Switzerland*. London: National Institute of Economic and Social Research.

Davis, R.B. and McKnight, C. (1980) The influence of semantic content on algorithmic behavior. *Journal of Children's Mathematical Behavior*, 3(1): 39–87.

Department for Education (1995) *Mathematics in the National Curriculum*. London: HMSO.

Hughes, M. (1986) *Children and Number: Difficulties in Learning Mathematics*. Oxford: Blackwell.

Jones, D.A. (1975) Don't just mark the answer – have a look at the method. *Mathematics in School*, 4(3): 29–31.

National Curriculum Council (1989) *Non-Statutory Guidance*. York: NCC.

Plunkett, S. (1979) Decomposition and all that rot. *Mathematics in Schools*, 8(3): 2–5.

Schliemann, A.D. (1988) Strategy choice in solving additions: Memory or understanding of numerical relations? In A. Bordas (ed.) *Proceedings of the Twelfth Annual*

Conference of the International Group for the Psychology of Mathematics' Education, pp. 544–551. Veszprem: Ferenc Genzwein.

Scottish Office Education Department (1991) *Mathematics 5–14*. Edinburgh: SOED.

Thompson, I. (1994) Young children's idiosyncratic written algorithms for addition. *Educational Studies in Mathematics*, 26: 323–45.

Section 4

PERSPECTIVES ON TEACHING NUMBER

This section focuses primarily on aspects of teaching strategy and classroom ethos. It suggests some activities for involving children in individual, pair or small-group work. Other activities suitable for teachers to use in interactive whole-class teaching situations are described.

Alan Wigley begins this section with an interesting discussion of the importance of language in the teaching of mathematics. In Chapter 10, he argues the case for an early emphasis to be given to the spoken and written *language* of number. He acknowledges the influence of Caleb Gattegno and introduces the reader to some of his powerful ideas, in particular his 'visual dictation chart', a device for introducing young children to the whole structure of the number system in one fell swoop and for helping them appreciate the overall regularity in the composition of the number system. He provides some practical suggestions for using arrow cards to introduce the notation system and how it relates to spoken number; the hundred square to improve children's ability at ordering numbers; calculators to develop their understanding of place value; and a computer program to enhance children's range of mental images of number.

Ian Thompson (Chapter 11) looks in some detail at the structure of the spoken counting word systems in English and Asian languages. The irregularities that exist in the second decade and elsewhere in English are compared with the logical regularity of the Japanese counting word system. Games are suggested which focus on the recitation, enumeration, counting order and cardinality aspects of early counting, and activities are introduced to familiarize young children with the irregularities of the number name sequence in English. These activities are to be delivered through the medium of a puppet, Miss Count, whose counting is not as reliable as it might be, and who is helped to perfect her skills by members of the class. The suggestions also provide a suitable vehicle for teachers to involve their children in some interactive whole-class teaching.

Greater use of the four-function calculator in the development of early number understanding is argued for by Janet Duffin in Chapter 12. She exhorts teachers to capitalize on children's positive attitudes towards technology. Letting children use calculators can generate discussion, which in turn can reveal a great deal about their numerical competence. In this context, the calculator is both a catalyst for mathematical talk and a useful diagnostic tool. She discusses some of the common difficulties highlighted by calculator use, and uses as a case study a school where the calculator has been fully integrated into the school's number curriculum – from the nursery class upwards! Examples of children's work and teacher activities from different school years are described, and particular attention is drawn to the school's approach to ensuring that the children do not become 'calculator-dependent'.

She describes the classroom ethos of a school operating a calculator-aware approach to the number curriculum, with its emphasis on teachers listening to and observing children in order to understand their thinking, and the children discussing, sharing, working collaboratively and justifying their work and their conclusions. She also suggests a way forward for teachers wishing to adopt this way of working.

In Chapter 13, Ian Sugarman briefly describes three different forms of mathematical knowledge: physical, social and logico-mathematical. He argues that, in addition to developing young children's physical knowledge through a practical approach to number and their social knowledge through an introduction to cultural tools such as standard number notation, teachers must develop children's logico-mathematical knowledge by helping them to appreciate the inter-relationships between numbers. He provides a wide range of extensible activities which will help teachers to achieve this goal by enabling them to adopt a 'teaching for strategies' approach.

Approaching number through language

Alan Wigley

Re-examination of some traditions in the early teaching of number

Before they can begin a serious study of addition and subtraction, pupils have to come to grips with the spoken and written language of the numeration system, needed for ordering numbers and for counting. The Key Stage-related programmes of study in the National Curriculum contain a discrete section on understanding place value. This is good because classroom practice often moves quickly on to computational methods, on the presumption that pupils will pick up place value understanding incidentally. The errors and misconceptions which occur frequently throughout pupils' school lives suggest that this may be mistaken and that they would benefit from more explicit teaching of number language. However, surprisingly few texts offer suggestions as to how this should be done. This chapter attempts to remedy the deficiency by outlining a structured programme. Subsequently, computational methods need to build more flexibly and sensitively on place value understanding. For many pupils, insistence on right-to-left working, with 'borrowing' and 'carrying', detaches digits from their true sense of place. Mental methods can be more meaningful because they often follow the natural order for reading numbers.

To begin, consider children's pre-school experience. Many people see early number work consisting mainly of 'teaching them to count'. Sometimes they count in the intransitive sense of the verb; that is, they recite the number names in order with no objects involved, just enjoying the 'tune'. Sometimes the counting has some associated physical action: an abiding image is that of a child holding the hand of a parent and counting from step to step as they bump down the stairs. Sometimes objects associated with the counting exist more in the mind, as in many popular number rhymes and stories.

All teachers of young children know about these activities and recognize their value. However, there are some reasons why a reconsideration of certain established classroom practices could lead to a significant improvement in the teaching of number:

1 A lot of time is given over to working with objects – sorting, matching and counting them – before pupils are fully secure in the number names. It might be better to treat counting objects, which involves a difficult act of coordination, informally in the early stages and to give more attention to learning the number names.
2 Sequential building from small numbers is natural for counting, but hinders development of place value understanding, particularly because of the irregularities in the spoken language of the second decade of numbers. Exploiting children's fascination with large numbers can help to reveal the overall structure, which is well within their comprehension.
3 Physical representations (e.g. base-ten blocks), introduced to explain place value, may not be as helpful as has been thought. There is growing recognition that place value is essentially a notation which has to make sense in itself, not through some external embodiment. Indeed, it can fairly be argued that place value structure is imposed on the materials rather than abstracted from them – certainly that is how such materials were invented!

Possibly the most significant advance in thinking in recent decades is due principally to Caleb Gattegno, who also introduced Cuisenaire rods and geoboards into this country.[1] In suggesting how early number can be treated as a part of *language* learning, he offers a way of dealing with the above issues. The following scheme of activities owes much to him, but incorporates other ideas as well. It attempts to show how, by working directly and systematically on number language, pupils' understanding of place value can be rapidly advanced. To be fully effective, it needs to be followed through systematically, ideally from when pupils enter school.

Language difficulties and how they can be tackled

Although place value notation is entirely regular, the spoken English language is not, and here lies the root of a difficulty. If, instead of '. . . , eight, nine, ten, eleven, twelve, thirteen, . . . , nineteen', the conventions in spoken English were '. . . , eight, nine, one-ty (i.e. one ten), one-ty one, one-ty two, one-ty three, . . . , one-ty nine', and if the decades followed 'one-ty, two-ty, three-ty, four-ty, five-ty, six-ty, . . .', then the sound of numbers would match the written form in being entirely regular. Significantly, the greatest irregularity is in the second decade, so that learning numbers in the natural counting sequence does not help understanding of place value at that critical point where it is first used!

Interestingly, the spoken language becomes highly regular for large numbers and herein perhaps lies the solution to the problem: introduce pupils as soon as possible to the whole structure, say of whole numbers up to 999, possibly beyond. Gattegno introduced a visual dictation chart for this purpose. The completed first three rows look like this:

1	2	3	4	5	6	7	8	9
10	20	30	40	50	60	70	80	90
100	200	300	400	500	600	700	800	900

By building up the 'tens table' in the stages suggested below, working for fluency at each stage before moving to the next, the overall regularity becomes apparent and anomalies in the spoken language can be made a matter for explicit discussion.

An important feature is the communal working, using a wall chart and pointer. Accepting that pupils will vary in their initial competence, the idea is to absorb the sounds through repeated recitation. Those less confident can listen and join in when they feel ready. This may sound rather traditional, but it is in fact, a powerful and enjoyable way of working.

The other great advantage of the tens table is the way in which it displays numbers in component form. Understanding this is essential to later computation work, where pupils need to be aware that, for example, 983 is composed of 900, 80 and 3. For making the transition to the standard compact notation, place value cards (a set of 27 cards corresponding to the numbers in the table) are the ideal adjunct to the tens table. Having been taught to say, for example, 'six hundred and three', pupils need to learn that it is written as '603' and not '6003'. Superimposing the '3' card on the '600' card with arrow heads together illustrates the correct notation vividly, helping pupils to understand that it is the position of a digit which alone signals its value. All numbers from 1 to 999 can be shown. For example, superimposing the following cards illustrates 500 + 30 + 8 = 538:

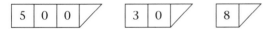

Place value cards are suited to individual working. So an effective lesson might start with some oral work on the tens table, continue with individual practical and written exercises using the cards, and end with some sharing of work done or more communal recitation.

Building up the tens table

The following describes the classic way of building up the tens table in a sequence of five stages, pupils mastering each stage before proceeding to the next.

Stage 1

On a wall chart of the tens table, first cover up all but the top row of numbers. Using a pointer, work with the class together. First, check that the pupils can say the numbers from 1 to 9, in order and at random:

1 2 3 4 5 6 7 8 9

Reception teachers often have a stock of activities related to this sequence, using number mats, 'washing lines', feely numbers, sand trays, etc. In passing, it should be noted that when comparing numbers in the sequence, positional language is appropriate ('before', 'after', 'between'), rather than the language of quantity appropriate to counting objects ('more', 'less').

Although some children have mastered the numbers to 9 by the time they enter school, it does require considerable effort, because nine words and symbols have to be associated, and none of them is predictable from any of the others. As a measure of comparative effort, only nine more new number words (or elements of words) are needed to reach 999, and one further to reach 999 999!

Stage 2

By adding the sound 'hundred' for '00', together with a convention regarding the conjunction 'and', pupils can now say a lot more numbers (the middle row is still hidden):

1	2	3	4	5	6	7	8	9

100	200	300	400	500	600	700	800	900

By successive pointing, pupils are invited to say, for example, 'five hundred and seven'. Working together, this is practised to fluency. Place value cards 1–9 and 100–900 can now be used. Exercises can be of the form, given a pair of cards what number will they make? Conversely, given a number, what cards are needed to make it? Pupils can make up some of their own exercises. When checking, get them to say the numbers they have made. When working on the tens table, sometimes invite a pupil to write on the board the number being spoken.

Stage 3

Introducing the sound 'ty', add these numbers in the middle row:

1	2	3	4	5	6	7	8	9
			40		60	70	80	90
100	200	300	400	500	600	700	800	900

Having learned these new sounds, build up to examples such as 'eight hundred and sixty seven'. Three-card exercises can now be given (i.e. incorporating 40, 60, 70, 80 and 90), in a manner similiar to the previous section. Some further two-card exercises should be included, as it is important for pupils to distinguish between numbers like 104 and 140, where the difference in the written form is between the zero being in the middle or on the right.

The conventional arithmetic signs for recording can be introduced at an early stage: '+' with the meaning 'and', and '=' with the meaning 'make(s)'. For example: 800 + 90 + 3 = 893. In this way, the superimposition of place value cards is linked explicitly with the operation of addition. When setting exercises, a case can be made for using question marks to indicate numbers to be found: $400 + 60 + 8 = ?$, $300 + ? + 2 = 362$. Some writers prefer to use a square 'box', into which pupils are expected to write a 'missing' number. It seems clear, and potentially less confusing, if they are taught that the question mark stands in place of a number which they have to find.

Stage 4

Three more entries in the tens row each require a slight alteration to the sound, e.g. say 'twenty' rather than 'two-ty':

1	2	3	4	5	6	7	8	9
	20	30	40	50	60	70	80	90
100	200	300	400	500	600	700	800	900

Proceed as before, again to achieve fluency. Extend the place value card exercises, with the need to practise three new sounds ($300 + 20 + 8 = ?$, etc.).

Stage 5

Finally, add the 'ten', perhaps temporarily adopting the sound 'one-ty':

1	2	3	4	5	6	7	8	9
10	20	30	40	50	60	70	80	90
100	200	300	400	500	600	700	800	900

Introducing the '10' draws attention to the most irregular part of the table in English. From experience of oral counting, many pupils will be familiar, by this stage, with the correct English sounds and may be amused that, when '10' is pointed to, the sound cannot be made until the units digit is identified! Temporarily adopting the sound 'one-ty' makes the pattern regular and can help pupils to recognize how conventional English differs: new words are required not only for 'ten', but also for 'eleven', 'twelve' and '-teen', the latter troublesome as a suffix because it leads to digit reversals. Exercises with all numbers up to 999 can now be set using place value cards. Related pairs, such as 161 and 116, promote discussion, which draws attention to the distinction between them.

The logic of the above sequence will be apparent, but it would be wrong to describe it as the only sensible possibility. For example, rather than introducing 'hundred' before 'ty', one might proceed row by row, temporarily regularizing the language of the second row ('one-ty', 'two-ty', . . .) so as to overcome difficulties. Either way, pupils appreciate how this helps to make the structure apparent, whether they are already familiar with the 'correct' words or not.

A further point also needs to be made clear. In offering an overview of number language, it is not intended to suggest that pupils should stop counting sequentially at 9! It would make no sense to stop them learning the correct 'tune' beyond that point. What the tens chart offers is an early exposition of the structure, so that pupils can make sense of it and see beyond those small but significant irregularities in the language.

Ordering numbers to 999

Beyond 1–9, nothing has so far been said about ordering numbers. For this, a large number square is useful, preferably in the following format:

```
    1   2   3   4   5   6   7   8   9
10 11  12  13  14  15  16  17  18  19
20 21  22  23  24  25  26  27  28  29
30 31  32  33  34  35  36  37  38  39
40 41  42  43  44  45  46  47  48  49
50 51  52  53  54  55  56  57  58  59
60 61  62  63  64  65  66  67  68  69
70 71  72  73  74  75  76  77  78  79
80 81  82  83  84  85  86  87  88  89
90 91  92  93  94  95  96  97  98  99
```

This sets out the numbers 1–99 so that each decade begins a new row. (The traditional 1–100 square starts each decade at the end of the row.) The teacher points to a chosen starting number, then up or down the sequence, with the class calling out the numbers in sequence. This activity can be repeated to achieve fluency with the counting sequence to 99. Because of the regularity, practice with numbers greater than 100 is largely unnecessary.

There are many activities to familiarize pupils with the number square. It is worth mentioning how useful the square can be at a later stage to illustrate the steps taken in a mental calculation, for example when adding and subtracting two-digit numbers.

Other activities

It is useful to supplement tens table and place value card work with other activities which directly enhance pupils' experience and understanding of place value. Some possibilities, using three different resources, are now given.

Number cards 0–9

These are sufficiently useful for all pupils to have their personal set.

1 Using them as digits, there are questions like how many different numbers can you make with three cards, and can you put them in order?
2 A game for two or more players involves a board where each player has a row of three blank squares, representing the hundreds, tens and units positions in their number. The cards are shuffled and placed face down. Taking turns, players take a card from the top of the pile and place it on *any* blank square. The object is to end the game with the highest number. Being able to place a digit in any space enables pupils to develop blocking strategies. Instead of the highest number winning, the rule could be changed to the lowest, or the nearest to 500, etc.

Calculators

Calculators are an invaluable tool for exploring how numbers work and for reinforcing ideas of place value.

1 Enter any number. Add 10 repeatedly. What do you notice? Try subtracting 10, adding 100, etc.
2 Put some 10-rods and unit cubes in a bag (e.g. Cuisenaire rods). Draw some out, record and add with a calculator, e.g. 10 + 10 + 10 + 4 = 34.
3 An excellent activity for reinforcement is a game called 'skittles', in which pupils first enter a number (e.g. 328). The object is to 'knock down' the digits to zero, according to some agreed rule (e.g. in order, smallest digit first). In the example given, it would be necessary to subtract successively 20, 300 and 8.

Computer program: COUNTER

COUNTER[2] displays a large digital counter on the computer screen. It is possible to vary the speed and the step, as well as other things. The program displays number sequences dynamically, in a unique way. Simple activities work well, with the computer under the control of the teacher. Using COUNTER enhances the images available to pupils and stimulates discussion of number structure and the regularity of the place value system. The openness of the program encourages exploration of large numbers, negatives, etc., and the sound facility can add greatly to pupils' imagery of numbers. Possibilities for early work include:

1 Run the counter and then stop it. Ask what number is displayed and what is the next?
2 Watch this number (pointing to the tens digit) – when will it change? Put your hand up when you think the counter is nearly at 100.
3 Run the counter backwards. What will happen when it gets to 1 or 0?
4 Can you predict the number the counter will show by the time someone has tied their shoelace? Run it for a lesson, recording the number shown at certain times. Can you say the numbers?
5 Set the counter running. Hide the display with a piece of paper. Stop the counter – what do you think is the hidden number?
6 Try different steps. Can you get odd/even numbers, multiples? Enter any small or large number, then explore patterns for different steps (e.g. 10, 100, 5).
7 Explore the sound option, e.g. listen to pitch of note for units digit. Set a secret simple step – can you guess the step just hearing the sound?

Some problems could be explored individually by pupils using the constant key on a calculator to generate sequences.

Extending the number system

Returning to the tens table, numbers to 999 are sufficient to provide a basis for exploring addition and subtraction. So the table would perhaps be extended with older pupils in the primary school. In fact, three additional rows can be introduced simultaneously. This requires only the addition of the sound 'thousand', triggered by '000':

1	2	3	4	5	6	7	8	9
10	20	30	40	50	60	70	80	90
100	200	300	400	500	600	700	800	900

1 000	2 000	3 000	4 000	5 000	6 000	7 000	8 000	9 000
10 000	20 000	30 000	40 000	50 000	60 000	70 000	80 000	90 000
100 000	200 000	300 000	400 000	500 000	600 000	700 000	800 000	900 000

When saying numbers up to 999 999, all that is required is to suppress the sound 'thousand' until, working upwards, the space between the blocks is reached. The computer program COUNTER is useful for displaying sets of large numbers. Pupils might work in pairs and set each other exercises to practise (e.g. say '785 932'). Also, they might practise writing some numbers fully in words.

It may be of interest to discuss even larger numbers. The American convention of a billion equalling a thousand million has acquired some currency in this country (where traditionally it was a million million):

000	000	000	000
billion	million	thousand	

Extending downwards, the numbers in each row are ten times greater than those in the previous row. Extending upwards, numbers are divided by ten to get the row above. This suggests the introduction of rows for tenths, hundredths and thousandths:

0.001	0.002	0.003	0.004	0.005	0.006	0.007	0.008	0.009
0.01	0.02	0.03	0.04	0.05	0.06	0.07	0.08	0.09
0.1	0.2	0.3	0.4	0.5	0.6	0.7	0.8	0.9
1	2	3	4	5	6	7	8	9
10	20	30	40	50	60	70	80	90
100	200	300	400	500	600	700	800	900

With decimal numbers, teaching the correct language is vital: each decimal digit is sounded singly, as with telephone numbers, e.g. 12.45 is 'twelve point four five'. Only when dealing with money is there a different convention: treating the point as separating pounds from pence, £12.45 is 'twelve pounds forty five'. Failure to recognize these distinctions can lead to errors; for example, pupils will read 0.12 as 'point twelve' and conclude that it is bigger than 0.2 ('point two'). Exercises with decimal place value cards, made so that the arrowheads dovetail neatly with the whole number cards, will help to reinforce the structure.

In summary, the tens table sets out clearly the relationships between the rows and columns of numbers in our system. Accompanying oral work establishes the conventions of spoken English. The place value cards provide a link with the standard written notation. Together, they help to establish an understanding of place value, essential to confident and fluent handling of numbers of any size.

Footnote: The importance of number language in addition and subtraction

Addition and subtraction are based on knowledge of complementary pairs. For example, opening both hands and folding three fingers illustrates how 3 and 7 form a complementary pair in 10. This arrangement makes available simultaneously these related facts: $10 = 3 + 7$; $10 = 7 + 3$; $7 = 10 - 3$; and $3 = 10 - 7$. Furthermore, simply renaming each finger 'ty' or 'hundred' generates results such as $100 = 30 + 70$ (reading 100 as 'ten-ty'), $1000 = 300 + 700$.

Understanding the language of number is at the heart of breaking calculations down into a series of steps. In mental work the key features are:

1 Left-to-right working, following the order of reading.
2 Preserving zero place holders in all cases; for example, by reading the '2' in 28 as 'twenty', not as 'two in the tens column'.

These principles can also apply to written methods with more digits. Thompson (Chapter 11, this volume) provides some illustrative examples of this calculation algorithm.

Detaching digits and working from right to left, leading to borrowing and carrying between hundreds, tens and units, have led to many problems for pupils in terms of understanding what they are doing. Using the principles outlined here, language and notation are kept in harmony with mental processes, so that pupils can calculate with confidence and understanding.

Conclusion

In discussion, teachers often agree about the misconceptions and difficulties which their pupils have. Believing in the powers of the learner, a thoughtful teacher will be prepared to question his or her own practice. But change is not easy, partly because certain practices become so embedded that it can be difficult to see that what is conventional is not necessarily the only possibility.[3] We owe a considerable debt to mathematics educators such as Caleb Gattegno, who not only asked questions but also offered alternatives which have been shown to work effectively and economically – based on one of his teaching principles, of seeking to 'gain a lot for a little'.

To end with a brief anecdote. A teacher, on encountering the tens chart, was sufficiently interested to give it a try. Some weeks later she reported back on a 6-year-old girl in her class who, despite previous attempts at correction by the teacher, cured a persistent problem of digit reversal for herself when she said 'fourteen . . . that means one-ty four, so it must be 14'. We now have available the means to achieve a secure understanding of the place value system, building systematically on children's pre-school experiences to give them an overview of the language of number. I can only urge you to try it!

Notes

1 The most readable introduction to the ideas presented here is to be found in C. Gattegno's *The Science of Education Part 2b, The Awareness of Mathematization*, published in 1988 (the year of his death) by Educational Solutions, New York. ISBN 087825 1952.

2 COUNTER is on a disk called SLIMWAM2, available for most machines currently in primary schools, together with an accompanying book of teachers' notes and suggestions, from the Association of Teachers of Mathematics, 7 Shaftesbury Street, Derby DE23 8YB. The disk contains other programs of interest in the teaching of primary mathematics.

3 A clear and useful paper is 'Laying the foundations of numeracy', by Helvia Bierhoff, published by the National Institute of Economic and Social Research, 2 Dean Trench Street, Smith Square, London SWIP 3HE. A comparison of primary textbooks in Britain, Germany and Switzerland, it contains an interesting discussion of approaches to mental work in continental textbooks, specifically two-digit addition. The elucidation of different traditions in other countries is illuminating.

Developing young children's counting skills

Ian Thompson

Introduction

In international surveys of the mathematical attainment of primary and secondary school pupils carried out over the last few decades, British children have consistently fared worse than their Japanese, Taiwanese and Korean counterparts. Foxman (1994) and Reynolds and Farrell (1996), in their reviews of the literature, provide detailed analyses of these international studies, and attempt to assess the factors that might explain country differences in performance. Smaller-scale studies in the USA have also shown that even at the age of 6 years, the mathematical performance of American children is significantly lower than that of Japanese children, and that Chinese 4-year-olds are able to count to a much higher limit than their American peers. However, one seemingly trivial but, quite possibly, important contributing factor that appears to have been ignored in these discussions concerns the structure of the counting word system of Asian languages.

Oral counting in Japanese and Chinese begins as in English by proceeding from *one* to *ten*. However, this is then followed, not by *eleven*, but by the equivalent of *ten one, ten two, ten three . . . ten nine, two ten, two ten one, two ten two*, etc. After *two ten nine* comes *three ten*, and the decade numbers (30, 40, etc.) continue this pattern up to *nine ten*. Within this system, the number which is one less than *a hundred*, for example, is *nine ten nine*. The structure can therefore be seen to be highly regular, logical and systematic, and such consistency and regularity must surely facilitate the appreciation and absorption of the recurring pattern that underlies this counting system.

The English counting word system, on the other hand, contains several number words which are likely to conceal the basic *tens and ones* pattern of the system. For example, the teens contain words which reverse the underlying *tens and ones* pattern: we say *fourteen and sixteen*, but *twenty-six, thirty-six* and *ninety-six*. This problem is further exacerbated when we express numbers in symbolic form, because the spoken reversal of the teens is not extended to the written representations of these numbers. So, even though we say the 'four' before the 'ten' in *fourteen*, we then proceed to write the number as *14*, with the 'teen' before the 'four'. Is it any wonder that many young children, when learning to write numbers, tend to reverse the digits in the teens, writing *41* for *14* or *61* for *16*.

English also possesses the two idiosyncratic number words *eleven* and *twelve*, which give no indication whatsoever of the fact that they mean *ten and one* and *ten and two* respectively. The problem is exacerbated by the fact that there are further irregularities: *thirteen* and *fifteen*, with their idiosyncratic pronunciation of *three* and *five*, do not even follow the straightforward 'digit-teen' pattern associated with the numbers from *sixteen* to *nineteen*.

A further important difference between Asian languages and English concerns the frequency of use of the word for 'ten'. In Japanese, the teens and the decade words all involve the conspicuous presence of the word *ju* (ten) to describe numbers such as *ten-two* (12), *three-ten* (30) or *nine-ten* (90), whereas English uses two differently spelled and differently pronounced variations of the basic word *ten*, namely *-teen* in the second decade and *-ty* in successive decades. Neither of these factors is likely to make it obvious to a young mind searching for pattern that the concept of *ten* is involved. In fact, a close scrutiny of Asian languages shows that because of the completely logical structure of the number word system, the word *ju* is used in ninety of the numbers below one hundred (all except the first nine numbers), thereby helping to reinforce the basic underlying regularity of the number word system. In contrast, the English word *ten* appears only *once* in those same ninety-nine numbers.

A further potential source of confusion in young children's minds is the irregular pronunciation of the decade words *twenty*, *thirty* and *fifty*. Because they do not have the regular form *two-ty*, *three-ty* and *five-ty*, as do *sixty* and *seventy*, these particular number words do not make it easy for children to see the way in which the words *two*, *three*, etc., are re-used in the naming of the decades. The words conceal the relationship between the decade names and the first nine counting numbers, a connection which is more clearly observed in larger numbers such as *sixty*, *seventy*, *eighty* and *ninety*. This relationship is greatly emphasized in the highly logical structure of the counting word sequence found in Asian languages. Wigley (Chapter 10, this volume) provides classroom activities related to these ideas.

It is also unfortunate that all of these irregularities occur in the early teens and decade names – *twelve*, *fifteen*, *twenty*, *thirty* – the very numbers that young children are experiencing and coming to terms with in their early number work at home and at school. This also means that English-speaking children have to memorize a long sequence of seemingly unrelated number names before the patterns become visible. Indeed, research does exist to show that there is a long period of months, extending to years in some cases, during which young children continue to learn the teen and decade names. English-speaking children have also been found to make more errors in reciting the counting words than do their peers operating with the Chinese regularly named sequence.

Even if it were to be found that this linguistic difference did contribute towards the inferior performance of English-speaking children, it is highly unlikely that any changes will ever be made to the counting words that we use. However, it is important for teachers to be aware of the likely difficulties to be encountered by young children learning to count, and also to be in a position to offer them activities and support for their learning. The rest of this chapter contains some suggestions of suitable activities for this purpose.

Models of counting

Maclellan (Chapter 3, this volume) describes Gelman's model for the development of counting competence in young children. Schaeffer *et al.* (1974) offer a different analysis, and develop a four-stage theory which includes the concepts of recitation, enumeration and cardinality. *Recitation* involves the ability to say the number words in the correct order on each occasion; *enumeration* describes the use of this sequence to find the number of objects in a collection; and *cardinality* is concerned with the numerosity of the collection. Pimm (1995), using an analogy from linguistics, distinguishes between what he calls 'transitive' and 'intransitive' counting. In English grammar, transitive verbs like 'to hit' or 'to eat' take a direct object (you 'eat' something), whereas intransitive verbs, such as 'to die' or 'to sleep', do not. Intransitive counting, therefore, involves reciting the number words for their own sake, whereas transitive counting is concerned with counting particular objects. Schaeffer and co-workers' model can be used to generate structured, interactive teaching activities for teachers to use with young children as a means of supporting their learning of counting skills.

Recitation

Reception teachers will, no doubt, have encountered those proud parents who insist that their children can count up to a hundred when what they really mean is that they can correctly recite the counting words, without necessarily having any idea as to how to use this sequence to count a collection of objects. Being able to recite the number words accurately does not, however, necessarily mean that a child can count properly, since there is far more to counting than the production of a correctly sequenced set of agreed words. On the other hand, children cannot even begin to count properly until they *are* able to recite at least the initial part of the chain. Knowing only the first seven counting words is of limited use if you are counting ten objects. Consequently, recitation is a necessary, although not sufficient, prerequisite for enumeration.

When children first learn the counting word sequence, they often treat it as a continuous sound string (*wontoothreefore . . .*), and only later do they come to realize that the sequence actually comprises separate words. For children at this stage of their understanding, the sequence can only be recited by starting at the beginning: it cannot yet be broken into and generated from an arbitrary starting point. For these children, starting a count from 'four' is beyond their capability. With experience, they come to treat the counting word sequence as a breakable chain, and learn to continue reciting from a given point within it. This is a necessary skill for children to acquire before they can progress at a later stage to using the calculation strategy known as 'counting-on'.

Introducing Miss Count

One way round the problem of generating meaningful discussion between an adult and young children when interviewing them for research purposes is to introduce a 'naughty teddy' or some such device. It has been found that children are more likely to argue with or correct the mistakes made by a puppet than they are to confront or question an adult authority figure. Using this research idea for teaching purposes can generate stimulating learning experiences, and can provide a suitable context for involving the children in some interactive whole-class teaching. The class is introduced to Miss Count, a puppet, whose favourite pastime is counting. Unfortunately, however, she is not particularly good at it, and the children are invited to help correct any mistakes that she might make.

The following suggestions for possible errors to be made by Miss Count are based on those mistakes which young children have been found to make when learning to recite the counting numbers:

- *one, two, four, five . . .*   (word omitted)
- *one, two, three, five, four, six . . .*   (words in the wrong order)
- *one, two, three, three, four . . .*   (repeating a word)
- *three, four, five . . .*   (not starting from the beginning)
- *. . . thirteen, fourteen, fiveteen . . .*   (error by analogy)
- *. . . eighteen, nineteen, tenteen . . .*   (error by analogy)
- *. . . twenty-nine, twenty-ten . . .*   (error by analogy)

When children spot Miss Count's 'miscounts', they can explain to the rest of the class why the puppet is incorrect, and the ensuing discussion can provide useful feedback for the class teacher on individual children's level of understanding. The activity also helps to improve the recitation skills of those children who are having difficulty mastering the sequence.

To make sense of the system, children need to appreciate that words such as *x-ty-nine* signal a change in the structure of the sequence, and that the sequence as a whole is a repetitive system (see **Nextup**). Even when they have come to understand that *x-ty-eight, x-ty-nine . . .* is followed by a different *x-ty, x-ty-one, x-ty-two . . .* children often do not know the order of the *x-ty* words. Some practice in reciting the multiples of ten is a useful way of developing this necessary knowledge (see **Anyone for Tens?**). Miss Count can also be used to focus on these particular aspects of the counting process. For example, she might incorrectly count . . . *twenty-eight, twenty-nine, forty . . .*, offering the wrong multiple of ten, or she could count in tens reciting the decade numbers in the incorrect order. It is also important that you ensure that Miss Count occasionally gets things right!

Nextup

Aim
To help children appreciate that a nine in the units column of a number signals a change in the decade structure.

Equipment
A calculator, set up to add one each time the equals key is pressed. Use the constant facility, following the key sequence 1 + 1 = = = = or 1 + + = = = . Children work in pairs.

Rules
Children need to be familiar with the fact that the calculator will count in ones each time the equals sign is pressed. One child enters a two-digit number ending in nine. The other child states the next number that should appear in the display when the equals key is pressed. A record is kept of player A's original number, player B's conjecture and the number actually appearing in the display. A successful answer scores a point and the players then change roles. The first player to score five points is the winner.

Anyone for Tens?

Aim
To provide opportunities for children to practise counting in tens.

Equipment
A calculator set up to count in tens (Press 10 + 10 = = = or 10 + + = = =).

Rules
Children can either work on their own 'guessing and pressing' or, better still, can work in pairs. One child counts in tens while the other checks that the sequence is correct by pressing the equals button. Children take turns, and the player reaching the highest number without making an error is the winner.

Extension
One child enters a multiple of ten and the other child has to continue counting in tens from that point. At a later stage in the children's learning, the teacher can adapt the game to include counting backwards in multiples of ten; counting forwards in multiples of any number; counting backwards in multiples of any number; counting in multiples of ten starting from a number between one and nine.

Enumeration

Enumeration involves assigning the correctly ordered number words in one–one correspondence with the objects being counted. Most children point to the objects that they are counting. There are 'visual counters' who 'point' with their eyes; 'digital counters' who point with their fingers; 'touch counters' who touch the objects but do not displace them; and 'physical partitioners' who move the objects where possible while counting them.

Since physical partitioners make fewer errors than children in the other categories, it is important for teachers to guide children to point with their fingers rather than their eyes, and to encourage them to touch and move the objects that they are counting. Both of these procedures will help children keep track of their counting, helping to eliminate some of the potential enumeration errors. Because of the complexity of this aspect of the counting process, mistakes can be easily made when enumerating. There are three different contexts for error: recitation, coordination and keeping track. To be successful in their counting, children have to coordinate the recitation of the number words with the physical act of pointing while at the same time ensuring that each object is counted once and only once.

Once again, teachers can make use of Miss Count to provoke discussion among the children concerning enumeration mistakes. Some of the errors that the puppet can make while enumerating a collection of objects include:

- getting the recitation and the pointing completely out of synchronization;
- pointing to one of the objects without saying a number word at the same time and then continuing correctly;
- saying a number word without pointing at a specific object and then continuing correctly;
- pointing at the space between objects and assigning number names to these spaces;
- coordinating the recitation with the pointing but missing out one of the objects;
- coordinating the recitation with the pointing but counting one object twice;
- correctly enumerating five objects and then saying 'There are six'.

Another error that children sometimes make involves the matching of the syllables in the counting number words to the objects rather than the actual words themselves. This can happen with *seven*, which is the first two-syllable word in the sequence, and which is consequently sometimes matched to two different objects. A child who counts one short each time whenever there are more than seven objects may well be making this error. Miss Count can do the same.

Children need practice at counting objects in different arrays: straight lines are obviously the easiest, while circles or random arrays are the most difficult. Counting out a certain number of objects from a larger collection is a demanding task, because the child must not only count accurately, but must also remember when to stop the enumeration. Some children have difficulty in keeping track of the objects they are counting. As discussed above, it helps if they move each counted object to a new pile. For fixed objects, they need to start in one specific place and enumerate in a particular direction. Miss Count can be used to simulate these difficulties and to provoke discussion about specific keeping-track strategies.

Cardinality: How many altogether?

Even when children no longer make enumeration errors, it does not automatically follow that they can count. They also need to realize that the number that they have assigned to the last object tells them how many there are in the collection, assuming, of course, that they have correctly carried out the recitation and enumeration aspects of the task. When asked for the total in a collection that they have just counted, many children will count the whole set again. They think that the answer to this question is the total counting sequence. If this happens, teachers can help by asking questions like, 'Do you need to count them all again?' or 'What was the last number you said when you counted them last time?'

   Another useful ploy is to refer to collections of countable objects by means of collective nouns such as 'family', 'group', 'collection' or 'party', so that the plastic pigs just counted are referred to as the 'pig family'. This may appear a little contrived, but it can sometimes help children to see their collection as an entire group as well as individual items. What we want them to realize is that once they have counted all the individual items in the collection, they are in a position to be able to answer the question, 'How many are there altogether?'. With experience, children gradually learn that the expected answer to 'how many?' questions is the last number assigned in the enumeration process.

Does the counting order matter?

Children who have counted a row of objects in one direction can be asked what they think will happen when they count them in the other direction. Some young children will count a row from right to left arriving at one total, and then count it from left to right arriving at a different total, without realizing that something must be wrong. Once again Miss Count can be used to simulate this situation. She can count a row of objects in front of the class and say, 'There are seven counting this way but only six going the other way. So there are six or seven depending on how you count them!'. You can learn a lot about individual children's understanding of aspects of the counting process by their reaction to this situation.

   Another activity involves making the puppet count a small collection of objects in different unconventional orders. An object in the middle can be counted first, and the children can be asked whether this is acceptable. Children can then be encouraged to count collections of objects in this way,

beginning the count with different objects. For children who find this difficult, it is easier to start with a small collection of different objects set out in
a line. Initially, the toy at one end is designated 'number one', and the difficulty is then gradually increased by varying the toy which is to be counted
first. A slightly more difficult task is that of making a specified toy 'number
two', preferably one that is not in second place in the line. This task can
obviously be made even more difficult by increasing the size of the number
which has to be assigned to a specific toy. Increasing the size of the collection adds another dimension to the difficulty factor.

Comparing quantities

The ability to determine which of two collections is the larger is central to
number sense. Very young children soon learn to recognize which of two
groups 'has more' provided that these groups are small. They have more difficulty with the word 'less' and even more with 'fewer', despite the fact that
the latter is more grammatically correct! However, the judgements of young
children seem to be based on appearances and, as we all know, appearances
can be deceptive. With small collections (up to five or six) children are sometimes able to judge automatically the number of objects in the group without counting them (known in the literature as 'subitizing').

   With experience, children learn that numbers can be used to compare
quantities. Consequently, they need to know how numbers relate to each
other in the number sequence, and to realize that if one number comes after
another in this sequence, then it represents a larger quantity (see **Dotty
Dominoes** and **No Go**). When they have developed this awareness, they
are then in a position to count one collection of seven items and another
of five items and deduce that the first is larger because 'Seven comes after
five when I count'.

Dotty Dominoes

Aim
To provide opportunities for children to work out 'the next number' or
'one more than', either by counting dots or by recognizing the pattern.

Equipment
A standard set of dominoes.

Rules
Proceed as for traditional dominoes but instead of placing equal dominoes next to each other, the players have to put down a domino with
one more spot. (The problem of how to follow a six was solved by a
group of children by allowing the blank to be used in this case, since
'There was nothing else for the blank to follow'.) Each move has to be

justified as a domino is put down. The player must say something like 'Five comes after four'.

Extension
Change the rules so that players have to put down a domino with two more spots (a blank can now follow five or six).

No Go

Aim
To give practice at selecting the larger of two numbers.

Equipment
A standard pack of playing cards with the picture cards removed.

Rules
The forty cards are shuffled and dealt face down to two players. Without looking at them, the children place them in a pile in front of them. They then simultaneously turn over the top card of their respective piles. The child turning over the card containing the larger number takes both cards. If both of them have the same value then it is a tie, and the game continues with four cards to be won in the next round. The winner of each trick must make a statement like, 'I have won because five is bigger than three', before picking up the cards. After an agreed time, the player with the greatest number of cards is the winner.

Only when children can successfully satisfy all three of Schaeffer and co-workers' (1974) criteria can it be said that they are able to count. By this stage they have actually achieved a great deal, but there is much more to come! They now need experience of activities where they have to find the total number of objects when two separate small groups are combined. Maclellan (Chapter 3, this volume) describes the way in which children progress from the 'counting-all' method to the 'counting-on' strategy. Ideas for developing this latter strategy can be found in Thompson (1992). Suggestions for the development of the more sophisticated strategies that usually succeed 'counting-on' can be found in Sugarman (Chapter 13, this volume), Wigley (Chapter 10, this volume) and Thompson (1989, 1990).

References

Foxman, D. (1994) The Second International Assessment of Educational Progress (IAEP2). In G. Wain (ed.), *British Congress of Mathematics Education* – Research Papers, pp. 95–101. Leeds: Centre for Studies in Science and Mathematics Education.

Pimm, D. (1995) *Symbols and Meanings in School Mathematics*. London: Routledge.

Reynolds, D. and Farrell, S. (1996) *Worlds Apart? A Review of International Surveys of Educational Achievement Involving England*. London: HMSO.

Schaeffer, B., Eggleston, V.H. and Scott, J.L. (1974) Number development in young children. *Cognitive Psychology*, 6: 357–79.

Thompson, I. (1989) Mind games. *Child Education*, 66(12): 28–9.

Thompson, I. (1990) Double up and double back. *Child Education*, 67(8): 36–7.

Thompson, I. (1992) Making games that count. *Child Education*, 69(8): 44–5.

The role of calculators

Janet Duffin

Adults and calculators

In a report which focuses on the standard of achievement of pupils in number work, and which is based on the inspection of the work of nearly 2000 primary school children, we are informed that: 'The skills of using a calculator were neglected in a high percentage of the schools; in only a tenth of the lessons were calculators used' (Ofsted 1993: 11). Why might this be the case? Some possible reasons include:

- fears, fuelled by the media, that calculator use will 'rot the brain';
- lack of awareness of their teaching and learning potential;
- worries that children will become dependent on them.

Many teachers want to use calculators in their classroom but do not know how to start. This chapter is concerned with helping teachers make that start.

Children and calculators

The general attitude of children to calculators is usually a very positive one. They take to calculators more readily and easily than do their teachers and other adults in the community who have probably without exception acquired what number competence they possess prior to the days of easy access to calculators. The children we teach are growing up in a highly technological age and it is our duty to prepare them adequately for future developments.

Having observed children using calculators and having been present as teachers learned how to encourage their use so as to maximize children's mathematical potential rather than inhibit it, I have come to the conclusion that, used properly from an early age, calculators can greatly enrich the number experience of learners. So how can we start to introduce calculators into our classrooms in such a way that our children can develop and maintain positive attitudes both to them and to the development of a number competence appropriate to their use? That is the crucial question.

> Calculators can enrich pupils' number experience

A simple way to start is to put a calculator into the hands of children and observe and listen to what happens. It can be done at any age and, if you listen and observe carefully, you will find out more in a few minutes about those children's understanding of number than you find out from tests or written exercises. For calculators seem to have a special quality in being able to generate talk among children and, especially in the early years of schooling, talk can tell you a lot about what they know about number.

> Calculators generate talk among pupils

Getting started with a calculator

I have worked with groups of very young children, keying in my telephone number and asking them to tell me what they notice. When I do this, their watching teachers have commented upon what the experience told them about their children's perception of number. Another idea is to start with a small group of children, giving each a calculator and listening to what they say to each other. This can be an enlightening experience for a teacher and I recommend it as an expedient to get you started with a calculator. But clearly, a more structured plan of action is needed for the longer term. The policy of a school in which calculators are fully integrated into the number learning within the school from nursery to the end of Year 2 is described below.

Case study

Calculators in the nursery

In the nursery they just give children access. Initially, the teachers were surprised to discover that the children appeared to know about calculators and that, in talking about them, they show that 'they know more about numbers than we realize'. For example, they know about telephone numbers and the number of, say, their granny's house. They tell their teachers that, for 858227, you say 'eight five eight double two seven'. So in the nursery, the teachers try to extend what children already know and help to familiarize them with the appropriate language and with the calculator keys.

Calculators in reception

In reception, some activities become more focused, using calculators and other equipment to familiarize children with the numerals. They even progress sometimes to making sums, from dominoes say, and checking them on their calculator, using the word 'and' for the addition key. Sometimes at this level teachers will replace the '+' key by the pasted-over word 'and'. The children are excited by being able to create a sum for themselves and then see it being recreated on their calculator. The creation of number patterns such as 552255 . . . on the calculator begins at this point and more formal work on their telephone numbers is begun, such as discussing the position of a particular digit in a number and the fact that there may be two or more of the same digit in any one number.

The real world of numbers and children's insights

At the reception stage, children sometimes show some quite fascinating insights. For example, one teacher spoke of a child who said 'I've put 99 into my calculator and then an "add" and then 7 and I've got a hundred and six'. The child shows clearly that she can read three-digit numbers, and reveals an understanding of number unusual at this stage.

It would appear that these children are already demonstrating some interesting things about the effects of calculator use at a time when, without calculators, we would not be expecting any child to be able to work with more than one-digit numbers. The calculator, even for such young children, allows them to relate their real-world experience – of large numbers – to what they are learning in school and, in so doing, is opening the way for them to see the connections between their real world and the world of school mathematics, something more often than not denied to earlier generations of children. However, it is particularly interesting to me that these children show their affinity to calculators through their ready acceptance of them as a means of representing a calculation they may have done in their head.

> Calculators can connect real-world and school number

Years 1 and 2: 'Tables' and a more structured approach

As the children progress into Years 1 and 2 in this school, the work becomes more structured, with activities designed by the teacher both to promote number competence and to help counter some of the possible sources of confusion for children meeting different representations of both numbers and letters.

In Year 1, the children begin to learn about the constant key. They learn that if you enter 1 + 1 = = = (or, with some machines, 1 + + = =), then each time you press the equals sign the calculator counts in ones. Thompson (Chapter 11, this volume) describes several games using this facility. Children soon learn to generate number sequences in twos, fives, etc., with some taking these much further than any traditional 'tables' would take them. 'Tables' in a pre-calculator era classroom can sometimes give pupils the idea that the tables only go as far as ten or twelve times but, with a calculator, children can readily see that such tables go on forever. In one classroom, a pupil had generated the three times table up to 3000 and another, on investigating the eight times table on her calculator said, when she reached 40, 'and the next one ending in 0 will be 80 and the one after that 120'. This shows how the calculator can bring out for users some important number insights that a more traditional approach to 'tables' can obscure.

Activities with the constant key to arrive at, say, the number 500 are introduced. Some children enjoy the sheer pleasure of pressing the key in quick succession and will tend to overshoot their target number. This is the occasion for probing questions, such as 'So what are you going to do about it?', 'How many too many have you got?' and 'How are you going to solve the problem?'. Sometimes children decide they might proceed by 'taking away twos' instead of adding them, thus demonstrating an intuitive perception of subtraction undoing addition. It is also an occasion for the teacher to advocate caution by observing the numbers appearing on the screen and advising the children to slow down if they wish to avoid going beyond the desired target. Both the overshooting and the caution give opportunities for children to develop awareness about numbers and the way they work.

Calculators are an aid to developing number insights

Some common difficulties highlighted by calculator use

It is also at this stage that children's attention is drawn to the differing representations of numerals on the display and keyboard of the calculator. As with letters, some children have difficulty recognizing and distinguishing between the digital forms of 2 and 5, for example. The teachers see this problem as one which can continue into Year 2 and work is structured to overcome such difficulties.

Reversals are a common source of confusion for some children. Writing 31 for 13 or 14 for 41 can occur with or without a calculator but, because the teachers focus on talking to a greater extent than is usual in classrooms where calculators are not used, they find they can better understand the difficulties encountered by these children because they are listening more to what their children say. So, at the Year 1 level, teachers accept 31 for 13 provided the child can tell them the number he or she means it to represent. By the time the child reaches Year 2, the teachers expect both correct keying in of a number and the ability to read it correctly.

Calculators can be a diagnostic tool for teachers

The teachers say that previously they had seen such reversal problems as a feature of the earliest years only, while children are learning to write both numbers and letters, and thought, incorrectly, that such problems had been resolved by the time children had entered Year 1. However, calculator use, and the consequent closer observation of their children's progress, has increased awareness of the complexity within reversals and alerted them to their likely persistence into later stages. The calculator, therefore, becomes for the teacher a diagnostic tool for investigating and trying to eradicate difficulties encountered in the learning of number.

Developing number strategies: The calculator as a facilitator

In Year 2, children's number sense is further developed through such games as 'I'm thinking of a number', and some ingenious strategies for finding the number in question are often devised: 'Is it the number after 3?', 'Is it the number before 8?', 'Is it an even number?', 'Is it between 50 and 60?'.

As their number sense develops, children will sometimes speak a sum in words, write it down and then key it into their calculator or, alternatively, will do the sum in words, key it into their calculator and then write it down. The calculator can provide a bridge to recording when children have some difficulty in writing down the calculation they have done in their head and described to their teacher. The very act of keying into the calculator the sum they have done mentally can help the children to record the sum.

The calculator can form a bridge between mental calculation
and recording

One girl was having difficulty in making a sum from what she had been doing. Her task was to start with some given number and to use arithmetical operations to arrive at a target number. In this case, she was aiming to get to 9 but had originally overshot 9 and got to 12. There was only a short pause before she said 'Oh, I can take away 3'. She had been asked to write down the sums she made when she did the task and it was this part of the exercise which was causing her difficulty. I suggested that she try keying each item of her calculation into her calculator as she said it to me. Again there was the slight hesitation as she realized she had got to 12, followed a moment afterwards by a confident 'take away 3'. She then wrote down her sum without difficulty, showing yet another use for the calculator – as an agent for helping children through the transition from the mental calculation to the recording of that calculation.

Estimating as a crucial skill for calculator use

It is in Year 2 that estimation begins to be significant as an extension of children's mental strategies. They are encouraged to make a prior 'guess' before performing a calculation; different guesses and the idea of 'best fit' is brought in, with wild guesses being discarded as unlikely. An assessment of how near each guess was to the actual answer follows the calculation. Mental facility is encouraged through work on number bonds, variations on 'bingo' and on 'pelmanism', the latter adapted to finding, say, the number that will go with yours to give you ten, an activity which can be varied to include similar number bonds to, say, 20, 30, 50 or 100.

Avoiding calculator dependence

A crucial feature at this stage is the game 'Beat the Calculator', designed to help children appreciate that the calculator is not always the best means of arriving at an answer. Two children work in pairs, one with a calculator, the other without, and they see who can perform the calculation more quickly. Changing round and repeating the exercise generates discussion about which calculations are better done without the calculator.

It is possible to use other, non-threatening expedients for helping children to see the importance of their own mental calculating. A teacher in a different school was working with a group of children to test and develop their mental competence. A child asked if he could get his calculator. The teacher's response was, 'Well, you can if you like, but I'm not sure it will help you'. The child did get his calculator but soon discovered that the others, working mentally, were getting the answers more quickly than he was – a much more cogent lesson for the child than being denied use of his calculator. It is, therefore, important to develop children's own confidence in their ability to perform mental calculations. Confident children are able to decide when a calculator is necessary.

The Year 2 teachers, in particular, are aware of the problems of calculator dependence and they watch carefully for signs of it. They notice those who always go first to their calculator before trying anything else; this makes teachers wary and they try to encourage alternative strategies. They are also wary of children who produce a number of 'right answers' with one or two which are inexplicably wrong; this too can alert them to the possibility that the child concerned is going straight to a calculator rather than using a mental strategy.

A report of recent research in mathematics education (Askew and Wiliam 1995) states quite categorically that open access to calculators does not lead to dependence on them. However, teachers would be well advised to make use of the strategies described above to ensure that this is indeed the case in their own classrooms.

To sum up, general progress in the calculator-geared school described above is through an informal play period, moving on to more formal work using and becoming familiar with the calculator, its display and its keyboard, leading to competent manipulation of numbers through activities designed to develop calculating strategies alongside calculator use.

A new way of working

At all levels there is a strong emphasis on the place of talk and discussion as well as that of developing mental and estimation skills, both based on the idea of building on the mathematics within the children rather than on the traditional conveying of knowledge and skills to be practised by the recipient. But, for teachers who are not used to this way of working, it is important to ask how to change from being a purveyor of knowledge to one attempting to bring out the mathematics within learners. It is essentially a matter of listening to and observing children as they work, and encouraging them to talk about the mathematics they are doing. Children in classrooms like those described are used to sharing methods with each other, and with their teacher, and they have to be able to feel that all contributions to a discussion are to be valued and that even mistakes – perhaps, especially mistakes – can be useful in helping to advance the learning both of the whole class and of each individual within it.

So how can a teacher become the kind of teacher who can make full use of calculators so that the mathematical potential of all their children can be realized? One answer to this question can be found in the outcomes of a national calculator project in operation in one Welsh and four English regions from 1986 to 1992. A lucid account of the philosophy underpinning this project can be found in Lewis (1996).

The CAN Project as a way ahead

This project was set up to try to determine whether free calculator use from an early age would produce a new primary number curriculum to replace the one in use throughout most of this century. This was the Calculator Aware Number Project, usually referred to as CAN.

Teachers in the project were asked not to teach the standard written methods but instead were to encourage the development of mental methods alongside calculator use. The decision to work in this way came partly from a belief that this would make it easier to judge the full effects of calculator use, but it was also influenced by surveys of adult practice showing that these standard methods were falling into disuse in the community (Sewell 1981) and the workplace (Fitzgerald 1985), where people were using calculators or self-devised methods appropriate to the task in hand.

The schools featured in this chapter participated in the project and, in the light of the evidence presented, it is important to think carefully about the teaching style the CAN teachers employed in their work.

As already suggested, the core of this new way of working was contained in the idea of listening to and observing children and coming to realize how they were thinking about the mathematics they were encountering. Teachers learned to listen to children, children to listen to each other and explain to each other and to their teacher how they were doing a particular calculation. A classroom ethos of listening, sharing, learning from talking and explaining began to emerge. Children worked collaboratively instead of hiding their work from each other; they learned to have confidence in their own ability to calculate, to explain and to listen to others explaining, as well as being obliged to justify their working or their conclusions.

For some teachers, this was merely an extension of a way of working they had developed in other areas of the curriculum; for others, it required a radical change in practice which was not easy to encompass at first. That it was the right way of working for a technological age in which learners using technology are, inevitably, in charge of their own learning in a way that was never true before, is something which we must learn to take account of in our own thinking about learning and teaching if we are to make maximum use of the technology at our disposal.

Being a competent teacher in a technological age

The key element of listening and observing, essential for helping children reach their full potential, can be quite hard to achieve for teachers to whom the idea is new. I would like to end this chapter with two personal stories about discovering the essence of the CAN way of working.

A colleague and I had been discussing the difficulties some teachers were experiencing in refraining from teaching the standard methods, which they saw as being so much more efficient than those devised by some of their children. They felt that if CAN was about sharing methods, they should be able to share *their* methods with the children too. Our conclusion was that, if we are to help all children to develop their full potential, then we must value and encourage their efforts towards this but that, because of the 'authority' of the teacher in the classroom, there is a natural tendency to want to do it the teacher's way. For this reason, if the teacher comes in with his or her methods before children have learned confidence in their own thinking, the teacher's way will take precedence and this might not be in the long-term interests of the children. The teacher must learn to hold back at first and this is quite difficult.

My very personal story, and a milestone in my progression towards being someone like the teachers who were successful in valuing and encouraging children's contributions to their own learning, was this. A teacher had been discussing with her children how to make subtraction of numbers like 199 or 201 easier than they might appear to be at first. The class had decided that a first subtraction of 200 would make the calculation easier and had to think how to get at the correct answer in each case.

I was working with one child who was using the expedient of taking away another 1 for 199, 'because 199 is one less than 200'. I was questioning him about whether, in taking away 200, he had taken away too much or too little, but I appeared not to be getting anywhere with him. Another child, sitting at the same table suddenly said, 'Perhaps he isn't thinking about it in the same way as you are and that's why he can't understand what you are saying'. This comment showed me that, instead of trying to draw him along my train of thought, what I should have been doing was to try to get him to explain to me how *he* was thinking; that way I might have been better able to help him to find a correct procedure for the calculation.

It *is* hard to learn to help children to their own way of working, but the CAN Project has shown us how successful this can be. In one LEA, a group of 116 project children took a standardized mathematics test for 8-year-olds and out-performed or at least matched a similar-sized non-CAN group on a majority of the test items. It is also, in my view, the right way ahead for the technological age that is sweeping us along in its wake. Children have less difficulty than we have in accepting it, and it is our responsibility to help them do what to them is natural but to many of us is a difficult path to follow. Anything less will be betraying our children's future.

For teachers who want to try to take up the calculator challenge, it is important to realize that this must be done collaboratively as a result of a school's decision to take it up. It will require much thought, mutual support and a great deal of discussion among staff to move towards a way of working that will truly prepare children for the future they will belong to.

References

Askew, M. and Wiliam, D. (1995) *Recent Research in Mathematics Education 5–16*. London: HMSO.

Fitzgerald, A. (1985) *New Technology and Mathematics in Employment*. Birmingham: University of Birmingham.

Lewis, A. (1996) *Discovering Mathematics with 4- to 7-year-olds*. London: Hodder and Stoughton.

Ofsted (1993) *The Teaching and Learning of Number in Primary School*. London: HMSO.

Sewell, B. (1981) *Use of Mathematics by Adults in Daily Life*. London: Advisory Council for Adult and Continuing Education.

Recommended resources

1 *A Whole School Approach to Developing Calculating Competence* by Ian Sugarman, Shropshire Education Publications, The Shirehall, Abbey Foregate, Shrewsbury SY2 6ND.

2 *The Teachers' Challenge*, an INSET pack published by the Mathematical Association, 259 London Road, Leicester LE2 3BE. It offers a resource for teachers trying to integrate calculators into their number work.

3 *Maths Talk*, published by Stanley Thornes for the Mathematical Association (first edition): now only available from Janet Duffin, School of Mathematics, University of Hull, Hull HU6 7RX. It contains many guidelines for using talk in the early years of number acquisition.

Teaching *for* strategies

Ian Sugarman

Introduction

I want to argue, in this chapter, that the shift in approach that is now demanded by the National Curricula of England and Wales, Scotland and Northern Ireland towards a mental facility with number requires a considerable re-direction of teaching strategies. Despite a popular belief that schools, during the past two or three decades, have seen a substantial move towards discovery-based teaching approaches, the teaching of mathematics has been spectacularly resistant to change. Ofsted (1994) reported an over-concentration upon the use of commercial schemes. These schemes abound with exercises to practise certain favoured routines for the four operations. Attempts are sometimes made to include examples of alternative strategies to practise, but there remains a clear message to the teacher that calculations are done with pencil and paper. More significantly, there is a strong sense conveyed that teaching arithmetic is all about showing children what to *do* rather than how to *think*. The concomitant of this approach is that failure to perform becomes largely a function of a weak memory.

The current concern with the development of mental skills needs to be seen as a plea for equipping children with a more generalized feeling for number. While primary school arithmetic was seen to be chiefly concerned with written routines of calculation, it may have been logical to pursue this through a behaviourist agenda – showing pupils 'how to do it', then getting them to practise. Now that 'a feeling for number' has been given greater priority, a behaviourist approach to the teaching of arithmetic needs to be replaced by one that recognizes the constructivist nature of arithmetical knowledge.

Kamii (1985, 1989) has distinguished between different forms of knowledge. The practice of counting out cubes, counters or fingers to effect an addition or subtraction is regarded by Kamii as 'physical knowledge'. Learning how to write this down as a 'sum' is regarded as 'social knowledge'. The mental process engaged in by children when thinking about the relationship between the numbers is quite different and is 'logico-mathematical knowledge'. Teaching arithmetic from commercial mathematics schemes, one may be forgiven for confusing what is merely an author's preferred style of recording, involving arrows, brackets, vertical arrangement of numbers, etc., for mathematical knowledge itself. The expectation that pupils at primary school will develop flexible rather than standardized approaches rests upon the conviction that, for the majority of calculations, it will be mental not written strategies that will be adopted. A crucial implication here is that the teaching strategies designed to facilitate the performance of written strategies may be counterproductive to those which facilitate flexible mental approaches. I wish to argue, with Kamii, that teachers need to switch from the teaching of social knowledge to the development of logico-mathematical knowledge.

Using structured equipment

Pupils in the first 2–3 years of schooling have been encouraged to use equipment such as counters and cubes to represent numerals. Alongside this practical activity has been the expectation that pupils will record the numbers and the answer in a particular way, usually in a vertical fashion. Only when set out in this way is the process regarded as being completed. At a later stage, there has been an expectation that pupils will manage to go through the process without the aid of the equipment, although they may well resort to symbolic substitutes, such as fingers or dots or dashes written on paper.

Conventionally, the teacher's role here is one of encouraging pupils to adopt a *behavioural* response along these lines:

1 Look at the two numbers to be added.
2 Count out the first number in counters (or any substitute, e.g. fingers).
3 Count out the second number.
4 Count everything.

This procedure eventually leads to starting with one of the numbers and counting *on* the other number (e.g. $7 + 4$ as $7 \ldots 8, 9, 10, 11$). The important consideration here is that the efforts of the teacher are concentrated on affecting what the pupils *do*, rather than what they *think*.

Compare this procedure with thinking about $7 + 4$ as:

A 7 (+2), (+2);
B 7(+3) = 10; 10 (+1) = 11;
C (6 + 4) = 10; 10 (+1) = 11;
D (4 + 4) = 8; 8 (+3) = 11.

In example A, the 4 in $7 + 4$ has been thought of as $2 + 2$ (a recalled fact), and used to make the process of counting 4 easier to keep track of ($7 \ldots 8$, $9, \ldots 10, 11$). In example B, the complement of 7 to make 10 is recalled ($7 + 3$). In example C, the complement of 4 to make 10 is recalled ($6 + 4$). In example D, it is a doubles fact that is recalled, accompanied by the recalled (or calculated) knowledge that the difference between 4 and 7 is 3, so that 3 needs to be added to $4 + 4$.

Figure 13.1 A set of coin cards

What might be the response to a slightly different sum (e.g. 6 + 9)? I have found that, even in classes where there has not been a deliberate effort by the class teacher to help pupils construct ideas about calculating, pupils often exhibit a range of strategies to tackle this sum. Some methods reflect the principle outlined above of recalling complements of 10 and doubles facts ((6 + 6) + 3), but there are others which have been found to be widespread, and exist independently of explicit teaching. Typically, the teachers concerned are unaware of their pupils' strategies and when drawn to their attention are impressed at their ingenuity.

Five as an intermediate grouping

Many children make use of a five grouping in the numbers between 5 and 10. Introducing 5 as an intermediate grouping before 10 encourages the principle of transforming numbers to make them easier to handle. For example, Michelle thought about 7 + 8 as (5 + 2) + (5 + 3). She described her solution in this way:

> There's 5 there [pointing at the 7] and another 5 there [pointing at the 8]. That makes 10. Then there's 2 and 3. That's another 5. Ten and 5 is 15.

The usefulness of this strategy is enhanced by the awareness she has already constructed about the effect of adding a number to 10, which avoids the necessity of counting. This powerful, labour-saving awareness is brought into play to great effect by Neil, who explains that, since 7 is (5) + 2, the 2 can be added on to the 8 to make 10. The sum, 7 + 8, has now been transformed into 5 + 10 and, therefore, is much easier to deal with.

There are various ways that teachers can help pupils develop the awarenesses that enable them to transform small numbers mentally. The existence of five fingers on a hand is no coincidence in this respect. Our decimal system undoubtedly owes its origins to this fact. Pupils come to establish an association between the numbers 6, 7, 8, 9, 10 as (5 + 1), (5 + 2), (5 + 3), (5 + 4), (5 + 5) by modelling numbers greater than 5 with hands and fingers. This can be reinforced by using playing cards with a 5 grouping, such as 5p coins and 1p coins (Fig. 13.1), or 'tile' cards, showing a 5-rod and ones (the sizes of yellow and white Cuisenaire rods) (Fig. 13.2), instead of a dice, to indicate how many spaces to move a counter in games like Snakes and Ladders. What children *see* is an image of a number, structured as a 5 and one or more ones, which is then interpreted as a single number to be counted out on the game board.

Figure 13.2 A set of tile cards

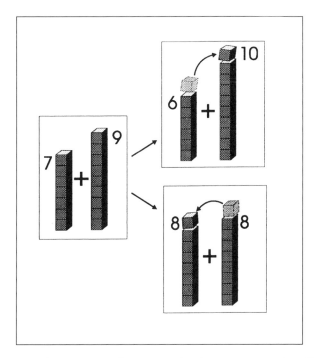

Figure 13.3 Transforming numbers to make them easier to handle
           mentally

Altering the numbers

Another strategy sometimes used by children involves an awareness that a
difficult sum can be made to look easy simply by subtracting a bit of one
number and adding it on to the other. For example, to solve $7 + 9$, Cathy
thought of it as $6 + 10$. An obvious way of demonstrating this transformation
is to model both numbers as rods of interlocking cubes. One cube from the
7-rod can be removed and joined onto the 9-rod. This idea can be shown to
be of particular value when any pair of numbers has a difference of two. Just
as powerful to children who know their doubles facts is the image of subtracting a cube from the larger number and joining it to the smaller to create
two identical numbers, in this case $8 + 8$ (Fig. 13.3).

I have now identified three distinct competencies: the recall of facts (e.g. the complements of 10, the doubles), the performance of skills (e.g. counting, partitioning numbers) and the knowledge of concepts and relationships (e.g. the importance of 10, the notion of a 'near double', the principle of transforming to retain equivalence). We can locate the source of some of the problems faced by children in the later primary years and beyond in these three areas. Clearly, an imbalance or weakness in any of these areas will restrict the range of choices open to pupils when attempting to solve addition and difference problems mentally. Of crucial importance is the awareness of number relationships, without which, knowledge gained in the other two areas can remain inert and wasted. For example, the ability to recall the answer to $5 + 5$ can only 'realize its potential' when it is appreciated that this fact provides a stepping stone to providing the answer to $4 + 5$ and $5 + 6$, if these are answers not recalled.

Teaching, therefore, needs to focus upon developing pupils' awarenesses of the ways in which our number system operates, and the ways in which their memory can be put to more creative purposes. The moments that pass after a child reads the 'sum' is the time when they need to consider how best to tackle it. For many children, this decision-making process has passed unnoticed and remains undervalued. Making it the prime area of concern is what teaching *for* strategies is all about.

So far, I have discussed some of the first ways in which children can move on from strategies in which counting is used exclusively to those which may incorporate counting within an overall strategy of transformation. Counting has been shown to be associated with the recall of a number fact where a subsequent addition fact is not known (e.g. in response to $7 + 4$, $4 + 4$ is recalled and the remaining 3 is counted on: $8 \ldots 9, 10, 11$).

Working with two-digit numbers

It is now appropriate to consider the ways in which pupils can be taught to extend this ability to transform pairs of single-digit or 'teen' numbers to all two-digit numbers. Many children learn to count up to 100 well before they learn how to add two small numbers together. This formidable skill arises not through the memorization of 100 different number names, but the memorization of only nine unit words, eleven, twelve, thirteen, two decade names (twenty, thirty), the use of -ty for the decade numbers and -teen for the numbers between 12 and 20. (A more detailed account of these ideas is to be found in Thompson, Chapter 11, this volume.) This, and the principle of re-naming the unit numbers with each new decade number, amounts to an impressive achievement, but a very different one from if we were talking of 100 disconnected sounds. It is precisely because young children have the intellectual capacity to combine the knowledge of a small number of sounds with a set of rules governing their use that the feat of counting to 100 is possible. Without logic and a sense of pattern at their disposal, they would have to rely upon a phenomenal feat of memory. It needs to be recognized, therefore, that being able to recite the number names to 100 is not equivalent to having a sense of the distances between any of those numbers. It is as if the territory has been charted but not explored. Exploring the territory of number needs to be a major goal for teachers in the first years of schooling. A game which can contribute towards this is called 'Going Places'.

'Going Places'

Designed to involve a group of three children, 'Going Places' uses the calculator as a means of helping children come to understand how the next number in the counting sequence is obtained by adding 1. It also shows that this principle operates whatever the size of the number. Kamii (1985, 1989) argues that children's facility with counting is a behavioural skill which needs to be supplemented by an awareness of the underlying logic behind the counting process: 'Numbers are learned not by empirical abstraction from sets that are already made but by reflective abstraction as the child constructs relationships'. 'Going Places' allows children to explore 'gently' the territory of two-digit numbers by adding and subtracting 1 or 2, in a progressive fashion. The calculator performs a range of functions:

- it demonstrates the means by which one number can be transformed into another one, that is slightly bigger or slightly smaller, by a simple, yet precise instruction;
- it demonstrates that the function of an addition symbol is to make numbers become larger and a subtraction symbol is to make them smaller;
- it provides a reference to how numbers look, and in the context of the game, how to write them;
- it gives control to children to direct the progress and pace of the activity.

A 'territory' considered suitable for exploration is identified for the three players; for example, numbers up to 30, up to 100, just over 100, in the 200s. An appropriate starting number is entered into the calculator, e.g. 16, 78, 92, 196 for the territories just mentioned. There are three distinct roles in the game, each of which is performed by one of the players.

Player A rolls a dice with the following instructions written on its six faces:

Player B enters the dice instruction into a calculator. Player C is a scribe, who writes the dice instruction onto a recording sheet (Fig. 13.4). Play progresses as the two players without the calculator attempt to predict what number will be displayed when the calculator operator presses the equals sign. When the calculator operator confirms or refutes the prediction, the scribe writes the new number onto the recording sheet ready for the next throw of the dice. While it is tempting to make an assumption of a direct correspondence between success at this task and an ability to count the numbers in a given territory, experience has shown that many children claim a facility with counting which is not matched by their ability to make correct predictions.

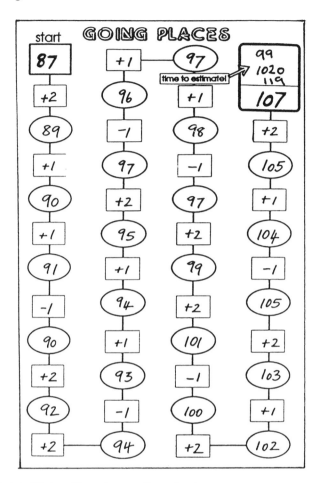

Figure 13.4 A 'Going Places' recording sheet

This would appear to confirm Kamii's point that the ability to name numbers in the correct order (a behavioural skill) precedes the awareness of how the 'adding 1 principle' operates. Playing 'Going Places', together with programming the calculator to produce the counting sequence, by constantly entering +1 and, subsequently, by the simpler +1 = = = =, allows children to experience for themselves the secret of generating consecutive numbers.

At this stage, it is likely that children see numbers as points along an increasingly lengthening number line. A breakthrough comes with the introduction of the hundred number square. Here they see their counting knowledge, where numbers are named in decade groups, given pictorial confirmation. The 0–99 square aligns numbers in one direction according to the decade (all the 20s, 30s, etc.) and in the other direction according to the units (e.g. 3, 13, 23, 33, etc.) and provides a wealth of investigative opportunities.

0	1	2	3	4	5	6	7	8	9
10	11	12	13	14	15	16	17	18	19
20	21	22	23	24	25	26	27	28	29
30	31	32	33	34	35	36	37	38	39
40	41	42	43	44	45	46	47	48	49
50	51	52	53	54	55	56	57	58	59
60	61	62	63	64	65	66	67	68	69
70	71	72	73	74	75	76	77	78	79
80	81	82	83	84	85	86	87	88	89
90	91	92	93	94	95	96	97	98	99

Figure 13.5 Recording the progress of the game 'Towards 100'

'Towards 100'

The aim of this game is to highlight the crucial fact that numbers that are 10 apart share a common unit. Each player has his or her own small hundred square but shares a dice, on the faces of which are written three 1s and three 10s. The game records the route taken by an imaginary dice as it travels around the hundred square towards 100. Players colour in the zero and take turns to roll the dice. After each throw, the dice number is counted on (either 1 or 10) and the new number *coloured in* (Fig. 13.5). Each player stops rolling the dice when a number on the bottom row (90 to 99) has been reached. Whoever finishes on the larger number is the winner.

After some experience with this game, children realize that counting 10 always produces a number which is directly *below* the last one. However, once this awareness is registered, their attention may cease to be directed at the number, merely its position. A way of redirecting attention to the actual numbers in the trail is to replace the hundred number square with a hundred square without numbers. Now the rules require the players to write in the numbers that the imaginary counter lands on (Fig. 13.6). Thus they now need to consider which number is, for example, 10 more than 24. 'Towards 100' confronts them with an important generalization that releases them from the burden of counting; that is, adding 10 to a number merely alters the tens digit, while the unit digit remains the same.

Thus far, the approach to teaching number has been confined to its ordinal aspect, thinking of numbers as positions occupied on a number line or number square. Many pupils benefit from the inclusion of a mental image of two-digit numbers as quantities. Two-digit numbers, modelled with rods of interlocking cubes, establish the powerful idea that a large number can be represented very quickly. For example, compare the time taken to count out 32 individual cubes with that needed to pick up three rods of 10 cubes plus

0	1								
	11								
	21	22							
		32							
		42	43						
			53	54					
				64	65	66			
						76			
						86			
						96			

Figure 13.6 Extending the game 'Towards 100' to using a blank hundred square

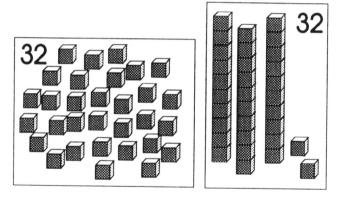

Figure 13.7 Grouping in tens illustrates the origin of number notation

two additional cubes (Fig. 13.7). The power of this idea cannot be overestimated. Practice at applying the skill of using this idea can be achieved through the following game.

'Four Throws'

This game can be set up as an activity to be worked on by children working in pairs or as individuals, each with their own board (Fig. 13.8). Initially, numbers can be modelled, as described above, using rods of ten interlocking cubes together with individual cubes. Each player takes a turn to throw an ordinary dotted 1 to 6 dice. After each throw, they must then decide whether

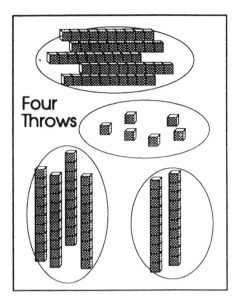

Figure 13.8 A 'Four Throws' board after four throws of the dice

to take that number of ten-rods or that number of units, which they place inside one of the ovals on the board. This happens four times, so that, after four throws of the dice, there should be four quantities of tens and/or units on each board. Each player then pushes together all the tens rods that are on the board and any single cubes to establish the total quantity of cubes. The winner is the one whose total is nearest to 100.

As children gain experience with this activity, they improve in their ability to make sensible judgements about whether to take ten-rods or units. This is partly because they learn to mentally calculate the outcome of alternative options before making their decision, and partly because they develop a greater sense of the 'territory' with which they are dealing. These tasks are designed to prepare children for the business of adding and subtracting pairs of two-digit numbers, through mental strategies. Thinking about the difference between numbers benefits from a sense of recognizing the relationship between numbers with the same unit digit. The next game provides this experience.

'Steering the Number'

Each player (or pair of players) starts the game with a list of random numbers between 0 and 100. For example:

- Player A: 4 13 18 22 24 37 40 67 72 80
- Player B: 7 12 28 29 34 45 51 62 70 93
- Player C: 1 3 17 28 30 36 42 64 75 89

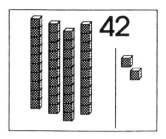

Figure 13.9 The starting position of the board in 'Steering the Number'

A starting number is represented by ten-rods and units, which are placed on a card (Fig. 13.9). The aim is to steer the number to make one of the numbers on a player's list. The children are allowed to do this by following certain rules:

• only one of the digits may be altered (either the tens digit or the units digit);
• a digit is altered by adding or removing any rods or cubes (but from only one side of the card);
• a number may be crossed off the list if it is made by any of the players;
• some change must be made to the number at every turn, even if it does not result in the making of a listed number.

Some children prefer to play this game competitively and others collaborate to try and make all the numbers on the lists.

With the starting number set at 42, Player A could either say, 'I'm taking away 2' (to make 40) or 'I'm taking away 20' (to make 22). If he opts to make 22, Player B is now able to make any of four of her numbers: 12 (by taking away 1 tens rod), 28 (by adding 6 unit cubes), 29 (by adding 7 unit cubes) or 40 (by adding 4 tens rods). It is appropriate for players to record each of the transformations in the game on the calculator. With the starting number displayed, they need to take note of the physical action (adding to or subtracting from) and the accompanying commentary supplied by the player, in order to press the appropriate keys which will allow the calculator to display the next number on the board. For example:

If the number goes from 42 to 22 ... $42 - 20 = (22)$
Then after the next change ... $+\ 6 = (28)$ (Fig. 13.10)

This facility of adding and subtracting multiples of ten to any number is a crucial skill when mentally calculating the difference between two numbers.

A common feature of these tasks is the active nature of the participants combined with the need for children to respond to a stimulus, generated by the throwing of a dice or the action of another participant. The tasks are also interactive, allowing for mutual support, which is of great importance in the context of a busy classroom. They involve the handling of equipment and, usually, an element of written recording, which allows teachers opportunities to monitor progress.

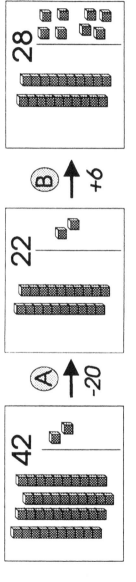

Figure 13.10 The progress of play in 'Steering the Number'

Discussion

I began this chapter by contrasting two different forms of knowledge and then went on to establish an association between these and two distinct teaching approaches. Teaching children to develop their own sensible methods for calculating mentally may well involve a substantial reassessment of teaching strategies. Teachers who are concerned to enable pupils to acquire the range of awarenesses, skills and recall of facts required for efficient mental calculation will find it helpful to consider to what extent they may be trying to achieve contradictory and inconsistent objectives. The use of equipment has traditionally been allocated a counting role. Pupils who have difficulties working out the answer to sums have traditionally been offered apparatus. This apparatus, such as counters or cubes, has done little to help them construct strategies that will release them from dependence upon aids such as these. This is because the visual image of randomly arranged (or even a long rod of) cubes leaves no enduring memory on the brain that can be distinguished from a quantity that is one more or one less than it. Pupils are effectively locked into a counting procedure from which they cannot escape.

Using equipment to teach a behavioural response or skill presupposes a degree of familiarity with numbers and the number system that for most middle primary pupils is highly premature. Teaching *for* strategies confines its use to the building of mental models of the place value construction of numbers rather than the explicit teaching of a pencil-and-paper algorithm.

Teaching *for* strategies is incompatible with attempts to standardize written recording, since this goes hand in hand with the encouragement of automatic responses to situations. The familiar page (or blackboard) of sums to practise a routine provides its own implicit message: 'Always do it this way, irrespective of the actual numbers'. Yet a prominent feature of competent mental calculators is their ability to *select* a strategy to suit the numbers involved. It is an unfortunate outcome of the standardization principle that many children are prevented from becoming confident in the handling of number because of the feeling that to deviate from a taught routine is mathematically unacceptable. It is a tenet of the teaching approach described in this chapter that to settle upon a method after considering an alternative is a major landmark in the development of a numerate being.

These ideas are developed further in a range of publications available from Shropshire Education Publications, The Shirehall, Abbey Foregate, Shrewsbury SY2 6ND.

References

Kamii, C. (1985) *Young Children Reinvent Arithmetic*. New York: Teachers College Press.
Kamii, C. (1989) *Young Children Continue to Reinvent Arithmetic*. New York: Teachers College Press.
Ofsted (1994) *Science and Mathematics in Schools*. London: HMSO.

The early years number curriculum tomorrow

Ian Thompson

. . . (continued) . . . 'Is there an alternative approach?'

Before discussing the alternative approaches recommended in this book, I feel that in the light of the preceding chapters there are questions which need to be asked about the 'set sorting, matching and ordering' approach to early number described in the Prologue.

Sets and sorting

One important attribute of a set is that its elements must have some definable property in common. However, Gelman's 'abstraction' principle (Maclellan, Chapter 3, this volume) states that one can count anything at all: the objects to be counted need have nothing in common. So in what way does the concept of a set help in the acquisition of this 'abstraction' principle?

If the language of sets is supposed to clarify issues, how does the definition of addition which is given in some teachers' texts – namely, 'Addition can be defined as the union of disjoint subsets' – achieve this clarification? How does this definition help someone who wishes to find the sum of the elements in two sets which are not disjoint? For example, a child may be trying to find the total number of letters in the two words 'boys' and 'girls.' The number of elements in the union of these sets is eight, since the letter 's' is in the intersection set. However, the answer to the original problem is obviously nine. The 'disjoint sets' definition is more likely to cause confusion, and generally adds nothing to a learner's understanding of what constitutes addition.

Matching

The reasons for the inclusion of matching activities in the early years mathematics programme appear to be two-fold: to help children to decide whether one set contains more or fewer elements than another, and to prepare them for counting (particularly Gelman's 'one–one' principle). Brainerd (1979) suggests that the ability to use one-to-one matching between the objects of one collection and the objects of another to compare their size is a relatively late development. Young children are actually more likely to use counting to answer the 'Which set has more?' question.

A very important aspect of the counting process involves the accurate matching of number names to objects, but why should children make any connection between the physical, written activity of drawing arrows from objects in one set to objects in another and the important 'one–one' principle involved in the mental activity of oral counting? It would seem much more likely that, just as they learn to talk by engaging in the process of talking – making errors, correcting these themselves or having them corrected for them – children will come to appreciate Gelman's 'one–one' principle of counting by engaging in the counting process itself.

Brainerd's (1979) findings might also explain the discrepancy between Piaget's conservation findings and the proven ability of many children under the age of 6 to make effective use of counting: an activity which involves an appreciation of the fundamental idea of one-to-one correspondence. Pennington *et al.* (1980) found that over 70 per cent of the 5- and 6-year-olds in his study who had failed a conservation of number test were able to make accurate judgements of equivalence when they used counting. Freudenthal (1973) argued that the usefulness of the idea of one-to-one correspondence within mathematics is no justification for its use as a criterion for judging a young child's grasp of number.

It would seem reasonable to conjecture that the ability to use counting competently shows an *implicit* understanding of one-to-one correspondence, whereas number conservation tasks assess *explicit* knowledge of the concept. One implication of this is that children who do not succeed on a Piagetian conservation task should not be denied number work, since they could well have a concept of number which is adequate for many basic numerical situations, and which could provide a sufficient basis on which to build.

Ordering

Putting objects in order of size or ordering events that take place during the day are useful activities for developing children's powers of reasoning and extending their understanding of the concepts of length and time. Involving children in pre-number work on ordering just because the counting numbers constitute an ordered set and because accurate counting involves the enunciation of the number names in the correct sequence (the 'stable order' principle) is a less convincing reason. Once again there is an underlying assumption that children will make a connection between ordering a collection of towers (either practically or with paper and pencil) and reciting the counting words in the correct order. There would appear to be no evidence to support this assumption.

Apart from the production of the counting words in the correct sequence, order actually becomes unimportant in the activity of counting, for, as Gelman's 'order-irrelevance' principle informs us, the actual order in which you count a set of objects is immaterial. The important idea is that no matter which order you count them in, provided that you follow Gelman's first three principles, you will always get the same correct answer.

An alternative approach

Based on my interpretation of the research findings discussed and the suggestions made by the various contributors to this volume, I have chosen to focus on just three classroom-focused themes that have been recommended as constituting part of an alternative approach to teaching early number. These three themes are:

- that counting should constitute the basis of the early years number curriculum and not the 'sorting sets, matching and ordering' approach;
- that mental calculation methods should be given a higher priority and should take precedence over formal written methods;
- that the use of a wider range of teaching methods should be adopted.

Each theme generates specific recommendations for action. In relation to the development of counting skills, teachers would:

- Use their knowledge of the irregularities in the structure of the language associated with the English counting word system and their awareness of the potential difficulties that may be experienced by young learners to help them master the number word sequence at an early age (Thompson, Chapter 11).
- Place greater emphasis on the *spoken* language of the counting word system so that they can help their children lay down a firm foundation for the development of appropriate mental models for oral and mental calculation (Wigley, Chapter 10).
- Ensure that children meet counting in as many as possible of the contexts described by Maclellan (Chapter 3), and provide activities to develop children's ability to count according to Gelman's five principles of counting.
- Involve children in counting for a purpose, and ensure that on all occasions the actual purposes of counting are made explicit (Munn, Chapter 1).
- Use the 'constant' facility of calculators to help children improve their ability to count forwards and backwards (Duffin, Chapter 12), and to count in multiples, in preparation for the early stages of learning multiplication (Anghileri, Chapter 4).
- Ensure that very young children are provided with practical addition and subtraction experiences, taking care not to formalize the activities too early (Aubrey, Chapter 2).
- Legitimate and encourage the use of fingers and counting procedures for the solution of simple addition and subtraction problems, and ascertain

whether their children are 'counting-all' or 'counting-on' (Maclellan, Chapter 3).
- Provide suitable activities and individual attention for those children who have not adopted this latter procedure, so that they can help these children attain this more sophisticated stage of strategy use (Maclellan, Chapter 3).
- Look out for those children who may become over-reliant on counting strategies, and help such children to learn some basic number bonds and acquire flexible 'procepts' (Gray, Chapter 6).

In relation to the development of mental calculation strategies, teachers would:

- Use their knowledge of the fact that, with maturity and experience of a variety of practical addition and subtraction activities, children will generally progress from 'counting-on' to the use of simple number facts (Sugarman, Chapter 13).
- Provide suitable activities to generate the learning of some doubles combinations and the complements-in-ten to facilitate this progression (Sugarman, Chapter 13).
- Ensure that mental calculation is given a high profile at all stages of the school number curriculum, and that children in the early stages of their learning are not pressurized into performing written calculations too early (Gifford, Chapter 7).
- Capitalize on their knowledge of the wide variety of derived fact strategies that children can invent to perform calculations, and openly discuss and compare the range of mental calculation methods they use, thereby providing them with opportunities to adopt or adapt methods used by their peers which they feel to be more efficient than their own (Thompson, Chapter 5).
- Provide opportunities for children to record in their own ways and invent their own symbols, but also ensure that, to facilitate progress, they learn to operate with conventional numerals and symbols (Munn, Chapter 8).
- Stress mental methods rather than formal standard algorithms for two-digit calculations (Thompson, Chapter 9).
- Ascertain the preferred mental calculation methods of their pupils, and use their knowledge of the most common 'user-friendly' written strategies to help their children develop written procedures which are closely related to their mental strategies (Thompson, Chapter 9).

In relation to the adoption of a range of teaching styles and the development of an appropriate classroom ethos, teachers would:

- Reject the 'deficit' model of teaching, which focuses unnecessarily on what children do *not* know, and adopt a more positive philosophy, ascertaining what their children actually know and then starting from this point (Munn, Chapter 1).
- Ensure the creation of a classroom ethos in which children will freely discuss their solution strategies with their teachers and with their peers (Duffin, Chapter 12).

- Strive to bridge the gap between children's number knowledge acquired out of school and that learned within school (Aubrey, Chapter 2).
- Capitalize on children's interest in technology by making the calculator an intrinsic part of the mathematics classroom, while at the same time remaining aware of the need to have strategies available for ensuring that children do not become calculator-dependent (Duffin, Chapter 12).
- Adopt a 'teaching *for* strategies approach', and develop extensible activities which can facilitate children's appreciation both of the connections between concepts and of the relationships between numbers and operations (Sugarman, Chapter 13).
- Make use of the calculator as a catalyst for discussion, employing games in situations where children are either working on their own, gaining immediate feedback from the machine, or playing in pairs or small groups (Duffin, Chapter 12).
- Deploy a range of teaching strategies to ensure that children become confident and competent in their mental and oral calculation. In addition to individual, pair, and small-group work, interactive whole-class teaching methods lend themselves to the teaching of oral work of this nature. These methods appear to be used very successfully for teaching mental calculation in Swiss, German and Taiwanese schools (Thompson, Chapter 11).

Comparison of approaches

I have only succeeded in finding one piece of research which actually attempts to compare alternative approaches to the teaching of early number. Clements (1983) devised a teaching experiment involving three groups of 4-year-olds. One class was taught classifying and ordering skills, the second was taught various counting strategies, and the third was kept as a control group. A 'number concepts' test and a 'logical operations' test were given as pre- and post-tests to all three groups.

The results showed that both of the experimental groups performed better than the control group on both tests, and the 'number skills' group significantly out-performed the 'logical operations' group on the 'number concepts' test. More interestingly, however, there was no significant difference in performance between the two experimental groups on the 'logical operations' test. This suggests that the children in the class that had *not* been taught using sets, matching and ordering activities had learned about these ideas incidentally while being taught various counting strategies. Clements (1983) drew the conclusion that logical operations do not necessarily constitute a prerequisite for the learning of early number concepts.

The contents of this book suggest that a 'counting skills' approach to early number is probably more successful overall than a more traditional 'logical operations' approach. As we have seen, the young children in Aubrey's study (Chapter 2, this volume) had no formal experience of sorting, classifying, ordering, matching or mapping activities, having been in the reception class for only two weeks, and yet, in general, they showed an unexpectedly high level of understanding of early number. These findings suggest that there is more likelihood of young children developing an implicit understanding of a concept such as one-to-one correspondence by actually indulging in the counting process itself, rather than by joining the members of a set of four cups to the members of a set of four saucers – a pre-number activity common to many commercial mathematics schemes.

The ability to use counting successfully and to create from this base a repertoire of mental calculation strategies which will later be supported by related written algorithms is likely to be more crucial to a child's development of an understanding of basic number concepts than the ability to sort, match and order sets of objects.

References

Brainerd, C.J. (1979) *The Origins of the Number Concept.* New York: Praeger.
Clements, D.H. (1983) A comparison: The effects of a logical foundations versus a number skills curriculum on young children's learning of number and logical operations. PhD dissertation, State University of New York, Buffalo, NY.
Freudenthal, H. (1973) *Mathematics as an Educational Task.* Dordecht: Reidel.
Pennington, B.F., Wallach, L. and Wallach, M.A. (1980) Non-conservers' use and understanding of number and arithmetic. *Genetic Psychology Monographs*, 101: 231–43.

Index

BEGINNING TEACHING: BEGINNING LEARNING
IN PRIMARY EDUCATION

Janet Moyles (ed.)

- How can beginning primary teachers not only survive but enjoy their chosen career?
- What can newly qualified and student teachers do to recognize and address the many complexities of primary teaching?
- What are the issues which continually challenge both new and experienced teachers?

This book sets out to explore with beginning primary teachers, and the people who support them in schools and institutions, some of the wider issues which need to be considered when working with primary age children and how these are woven into the broad framework of teaching and teachers' own learning. Cameos and examples of classroom practice help to illustrate the many different aspects of teaching: what it is to be an effective and competent teacher; classroom processes such as planning, observation and assessment; the variety of ways in which children learn and develop thinking and skills; social interactions and support networks; equal opportunities; and 'in loco parentis' responsibilities.

Written in an accessible style, the aim throughout is to offer guidance and encouragement in the challenging and complex task of primary school teaching.

Contents
Introduction – Part 1: Teaching to learn – Do you really want to cope with thirty lively children and become an effective primary teacher? – The classroom as a teaching and learning context – Observation in the primary classroom – Competence-based teacher education – Part 2: Learning to teach – Primary children and their learning potential – Planning for learning – children's and teachers – Developing investigative thinking and skills in children – Developing thinking and skills in the arts – Developing oracy and imaginative skills in children through storytelling – Developing children's social skills in the classroom – Developing writing skills in the primary classroom – Part 3: Responsibilities, roles and relationships – Assessing, monitoring and recording children's progress and achievement – Equal opportunities in practice – Working with experienced others in the school – Primary teachers and the law – Concluding remarks – Index.

Contributors
Tim Brighouse, Martin Cortazzi, Maurice Galton, Barbara Garner, Linda Hargreaves, Jane Hislam, Morag Hunter-Carsch, Tina Jarvis, Neil Kitson, Mark Lofthouse, Sylvia McNamara, Roger Merry, Janet Moyles, Wendy Suschitzky, David Turner, Martin Wenham.

288pp   0 335 19435 4 (Paperback)   0 335 19436 2 (Hardback)

ORGANIZING FOR LEARNING IN THE PRIMARY CLASSROOM
A BALANCED APPROACH TO CLASSROOM MANAGEMENT

Janet R. Moyles

What is it that underlies classroom organization, routines, rules, structures and daily occurrences? What are the prime objectives and what influences the decisions of teachers and children? What is it useful for teachers to consider when contemplating the issues of classroom management and organization? What do different practices have to offer?

Organizing for Learning in the Primary Classroom explores the whole range of influences and values which underpin *why* teachers do *what* they do in the classroom context and what these mean to children and others. Janet Moyles examines teaching and learning styles, children's independence and autonomy, coping with children's differences, the physical classroom context and resources, time management and ways of involving others in the day-to-day organization. Practical suggestions are given for considering both the functional and aesthetic aspects of the classroom context. Opportunities are provided for teachers to reflect on their own organization and also consider innovative and flexible ways forward to deal with new and ever increasing demands on their time and sanity!

This book is to be highly recommended for all primary school teachers...

(Management in Education)

...indispensable to courses in initial teacher education and to providers of inset.

(Child Education)

Janet Moyles brings her long experience of the primary school to *Organizing for Learning in the Primary Classroom*...I particularly like the attention she gives to the physical environment, giving lots of advice about arrangements of furniture and the role of the teacher's desk...

(The Times Educational Supplement)

Contents
Introduction: Polarizations and balance – Teachers and teaching: beliefs and values – The learning environment: organizing the classroom context – The children and their learning needs: balancing individual and whole class approaches – Grouping children for teaching and learning: providing equal opportunities and promoting appropriate behaviour – Time for teaching and learning – Deploying adult help effectively in the classroom: delegation and responsibility – Evaluating classroom organization and management – Conclusion: the primary classroom, a place and a time – References – Index.

208pp   0 335 15659 2 (Paperback)   0 335 15660 6 (Hardback)·